FORD
HOT RODS

DAIN GINGERELLI

MBI Publishing Company

First published in 1998 by MBI Publishing Company, 729 Prospect Avenue, PO Box 1, Osceola, WI 54020-0001 USA.

MBI Publishing Company books are also available at discounts in bulk quantity for industrial or sales-promotional use. For details write to Special Sales Manager at Motorbooks International Wholesalers & Distributors, 729 Prospect Avenue, PO Box 1, Osceola, WI 54020-0001 USA.

Library of Congress Cataloging-in-Publication Data

Gingerelli, Dain.
     Ford hotrods/ Dain Gingerelli.
          p. cm.-- (Enthusiast color series)
     Includes index.
     ISBN 0-7603-0475-0 (pbk. : alk. paper)
     1. Ford automobile--Customizing-- United States--History. 2. Hot rods-- United States--History. I.Title II. Series.
TL215.F7G52   1998
  629.227'6--dc21   98-3922

Text by Dain Gingerelli
Photos by Dain Gingerelli unless credited otherwise

Edited by Paul Johnson
Designed by Tom Heffron

Printed in Hong Kong through World Print, Ltd.

On the front cover:
Tradition runs deep with this A-V8 roadster. Originally built in 1940 by Herman LeHam, the immaculate 1929 Ford highboy is now owned by Tom Leonardo Sr., who bought it in 1971.

On the frontispiece:
A popular performance trick was to mount a pair of Stromberg 97 two-barrel carbs atop a Ford flathead V-8.

On the title page:
Malt shops and drive-in restaurants were favorite hang-outs for hot rodders. Dennis Love takes time out for a quick burger, fries and Coke inside, while his flathead-powered '27 roadster cools its heels in the parking stall.

On the back cover:
Wayne Hartman's 1932 full-fender coupe defines the timeless look of a traditional Ford hot rod. A tan leather interior dressed with classic instrumentation complements the hand rubbed black lacquer paint. Under the Deuce coupe's hood sits a flathead mill with Navarro heads, Tattersfield manifold, and two Stromberg 97 carbs.

CONTENTS

ACKNOWLEDGMENTS

As a moto-journalist I'm supposed to maintain objectivity in my work. However, I'm also a hot rod enthusiast, one who harbors unrestrained bias toward traditional-style Ford hot rods. These are the cars that I was exposed to when I was a young boy growing up in the Midwest during the early 1960s. At that time my brother, Alan, and I built and accumulated what amounted to a miniature car show of AMT 3-in-1 model car kits. Many of the model cars we built resembled the hot rods in this book.

Several "car guys"—in their own ways—helped me with this book. Thanks to: Alan Gingerelli; Gary Moline, Tom Leonardo Sr., Tom Leonardo Jr., Nick Leonardo, and their father and grandfather Frank Leonardo for their enthusiasm and friendship; Gene Story for exposing me to hot rods other than traditional-style Fords; Joe Kress, whose editorial insight at *American Rodder* magazine is refreshing encouragement that work should—and can—be fun; and to hot rod magazine editors past and present whose dedication and hard work ensures the longevity of the cars that I truly enjoy.

Thanks also to Al Voegtly, who rummaged through his old scrapbook in search of aging black-and-white photos that showed first-hand the pioneer days of hot-rodding. Also my appreciation to the librarians at the San Diego Automotive Museum (San Diego, California) and the Towe Ford Museum of Automotive History (Sacramento, California).

Furthermore, this book would be incomplete without mentioning my wife, Donna, and our two boys, Kyle and Christopher. Thanks for enduring more car shows and rod runs than you really cared to attend. The three of you are an integral part of my life. Your love and support is beyond description.

Finally, hearty thanks to enthusiasts the world over who enjoy and appreciate a style of hot rod that essentially started the movement that we call hot rodding. Specifically, I thank every hot rod owner whose car appeared in this book; your patience and cooperation is valued.

In memory of Mike Griffin, a thoughtful hot rodder, discreet confidant, and a good friend.

INTRODUCTION

Nobody in particular invented the hot rod car. Nor can the term "hot rod" be traced to a single source; however, it gained popularity and widespread acceptance in 1948 when *Hot Rod* magazine was first published.

Before that time hot rods were described in a number of ways. As far back as the 1920s hot rodders referred to their cars as "bugs" and "soup jobs." During the following decade, racers on the southern California dry lake beds coined the phrase "hot irons." Later, when the Ford flathead V-8 became a viable source of speed, the hot rods were called "gow jobs," a term that arose from the ongoing feud between owners of four-cylinder engines and the new V-8. The V-8 crowd was fond

Triple A goodness: This trio of Model A roadsters belong to Tom Leonardo Sr., and his son, Tom Jr. The full-fendered '31 in the foreground was purchased by Tom Sr. in 1964 when he was 12 years old. Price: $300. The shiny '29 in the background was formerly owned by noted cam builder, Racer Brown. The primered '30 with red scallops is Tom Jr.'s daily driver.

of saying: "four to plow, eight to gow," thus the expression gow job.

The evolutionary process of the hot rod has its origins before World War I when young men were known to strip their cars of fenders and extemporaneous parts to reduce weight and improve performance. This practice eventually led to organized races, and by the 1930s automobile racing had grown in popularity throughout America, blossoming into a bonafide sport. One of the more celebrated forms of competition was dirt-track racing, taking place on oval-shaped raceways that typically measured between a quarter-mile and a half-mile in length.

As enthusiasm swelled for dirt-track racing, permanent facilities were built to supplement the state fair events. Usually the racing focused on two specialized groups of race cars: open-wheel champ cars and midgets. But a more grass-roots form of racing also emerged during this era. It was the modified dirt-track roadsters.

The modified dirt-track roadsters were, in essence, stripped-down street cars. The most popular were Ford's Model T and, later, the Model A.

Hot rods often were driven by their owners to the race track, where the cars were prepped for competition. By removing the car's fenders and bumpers, the open-top car readily transformed into a nimble (by comparison), lightweight racer.

Beyond those changes, the major difference between a modified roadster and a typical street car was found in the speed equipment under the hood. (That is, if the hood wasn't removed during the car's transformation!) Popular speed equipment for modifieds included multiple-carb intake manifolds, steel-tube exhaust headers, high-lift camshafts, multi-lift valve adjustments, even overhead-valve

Looking much like a hot rod club of the 1940s, the Shifters were formed several years ago, in the spirit of the old days. Club rules state that their cars must be made of steel—no fiberglass—and they must be styled in the traditional manner. "We want rat rods," said one member. "No high-zoot stuff."

(OHV) conversions for the flathead four-cylinder Fords that dominated the class. These modified roadsters helped spawn the early hot rod movement.

About the same time that oval-track racing became a mainstay in America, dry lake bed automobile racing was establishing a foothold in southern California.

The enormous expanse of flat, hard-packed surface made the dry lakes ideal for straight-line racing. And when the racers discovered this phenomena, local race clubs rushed to the desert, promoting their own weekend-long, top-speed contests.

Early dry lake speed events allowed wild hot rod competitions. Sometimes as many as a dozen

Early 1946, and the war is over. Almost immediately hot rodders returned to their cars and racing. Here Al Voegtly (left) and his shipmate Bob Fredricks, stand in front of Al's 1930 highboy. Al was a member of the Clutchers, who raced at El Mirage Dry Lake. Photo by Al Voegtly, Tom Leonardo Sr. collection.

Al Voegtly's 1930 roadster, like many hot rods built during the 1940s, was driven on the street and raced at the dry lakes. It ran 120.96 mph at El Mirage during the October meet in 1948. Photo by Al Voegtly, Tom Leonardo Sr. collection.

hot rods—running 12 abreast—would follow a pace car across the start line. Once they crossed the start line, the speed contest became a free for all. A more refined method was developed by 1938 when the Southern California Timing Association (SCTA) was formed. The SCTA's early format was to allow each car two solo, timed, qualified passes.

The racing became even more competitive when, shortly after World War II, the Crocker Timer was born. Dry lakes racing took on a new dimension as speeds became more precisely measured.

Like their oval-track counterparts, the dry-lakes racers adapted a variety of modifications to their cars to improve top speed. And, like the dirt-trackers, the lakesters stripped their cars of useless sheet metal to minimize wind resistance and reduce weight.

Most of all, these racers tinkered with their engines' parts. As a result the speed-equipment industry grew up and flourished in the region. Men such as George Riley, Vic Edelbrock Sr., Phil Weiand, Kong Jackson, Ed Winfield, Ed Iskenderian, and Eddie Meyer founded speed-equipment companies on the needs of the young racers who hungered for performance.

Automobile racing at this level was pretty much a blue-collar sport. The entry list for both racing venues was comprised mainly of affordable cars like

Plymouths, Chevrolets, and . . . Fords.

Ford would ultimately prove to be the most popular choice. A major factor was the sheer numbers. During the early days of racing, the venerable, lightweight Model T was both plentiful and very affordable. A host of Model T engine performance products was offered by vendors such as Frontenac, Winfield, and Rajo. They helped the new speed-equipment market grow.

The Model A proved just as race worthy as the Model T, even though it was slightly larger and heavier. Because the Model A four-cylinder engine resembled the Model T engine, the speed-equipment industry easily adapted its wares to the new-generation Ford, once again making it a popular choice for racers.

Three members of the Clutchers, a hot rod club formed in Orange County, California, shortly after World War II, pose with their highboy roadsters. The Model A at the left, with its chopped windshield and '32 grille, is a typical example of a traditional hot rod from the period. Photo by Al Voegtly, Tom Leonardo Sr. collection.

A leading builder of high-performance parts during the early years of rodding was Ed Winfield. This pair of Winfield Model S carburetors sit on a Model A engine with a Riley 4-port overhead valve conversion. The engine powers a 60-year-old champ car, currently owned by collector Dick Fitzek.

But what really solidified Ford's presence in hot rod lore was when Henry Ford introduced his lightweight flathead V-8 in 1932. Almost overnight the racers and rodders had an engine that offered more speed potential than the venerable four-cylinder Ford, yet like its diminutive stable mate, the V-8 was affordable. Now the racers—and the pioneer hot rodders who emerged from those dirt tracks and Southern California dry lakes—had access to a powerful, economical engine for their sport.

With the introduction of the flathead V-8, Ford remained an integral part of hot rodding for many years. The flathead Ford became the engine of choice among dry lakes racers and hot rodders, and its four-banger sibling continued to be a popular choice as well. Ford cars were clearly the cornerstone of American hot rodding.

The sport of hot rodding evolved as much from the race track as it did the streets and roadways of America. An example of early racers is this '32 Ford, built by Scott DaPron. He based the car on a similar highboy that his father and grandfather raced at the Gilmore Cup races in 1934.

Early-day hot rodders quite often used military surplus equipment for their cars. This seat is from a World War II bomber. The gloves, leather cap and goggles are authentic 1930s apparel.

Hot rod styles have changed over the years, giving way to a multitude of trends and fashions. Various factors dictated those styling trends. The most notable are: a marked distinction between racing and rodding, the growth and popularity of custom car shows, and the lifestyles and attitudes of the hot rod builders and car owners.

While rodding shared similarities with dry lake and dirt track racing, rodders eventually branched out to other activities such as drag racing, car shows, and reliability runs. By the early fifties, the rift between dirt track racers and rodders had grown even more acute. For that was when dirt tack racing

Sixty years ago there wasn't much of a high-performance aftermarket, so hot rodders used what they could find, such as this tachometer that was built by a company in Stamford, Connecticut.

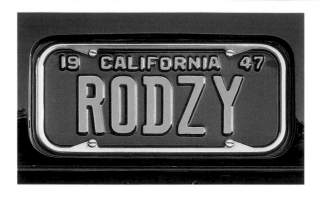

No, they didn't have personalized license plates in 1947. The "Rodzy" plate was fashioned for Mark Morton's 1929 highboy roadster that was styled after a scale-model tether car racer marketed by the Rodzy toy company before World War II.

For many hot rod enthusiasts there's only one car maker—Ford. Manufacturer's tags such as this were attached to firewalls of early Fords.

Only the open-top cars are allowed to park in the main lot. Consequently, you find yourself awash in a sea of drop-top beauty.

became a more specialized sport, even more so than it had during the twenties, thirties and the immediate postwar years. The high cost of racing eventually found its way into drag racing and dry lakes racing, too. And with specialization came higher costs to remain competitive on the track. Consequently, hot rodders unwilling or unable to spend the money necessary to compete at the track dropped out of racing, focusing attention instead to their hot rods' physical appearances and aesthetic beauty.

This shift away from racing also led to the growth and popularity of custom car shows. Chrome parts and flashy paint jobs became hot rodding's trademark in the fifties. By the seventies "Fad T-bucket" roadsters sporting artistic murals and spider-web paint jobs, and tall canvas tops, dominated the scene. By the seventies and early eighties, hot rodding had turned into a fashion statement of sorts.

Eventually, the fad T-buckets and two-tone hot rods (soon to be called "street rods") were supplanted by the "smoothie" look of the eighties. As the name suggests, the smoothie hot rod was a style practically void of extemporaneous chrome parts and protruding pieces. Running boards were filled and "smoothed." Bumpers were removed. Door handles were "shaved." And windshield posts and mirror stanchions were painted to match the body.

One styling treatment has remained an integral part of hot rodding. Rodders today refer to this style as the "nostalgic look," the "timeless look," or the "traditional look."

While there are no specific rules to dictate what the traditional look should be, most rodders agree on several points about "the look." Foremost, it should be timeless. When you look at the hot rod, you should not be able to discern whether it was built five days ago or five decades ago. Second, a true traditional hot rod should be based on a Ford. Not just any Ford, but one that was offered by the Ford Motor Company back in the early days of rodding.

That means it should be a Model T, Model A, Model B, or in some instances Fords produced between 1933 and 1941, and in extreme cases the "fat-fendered" Fords built during the immediate postwar years. Finally, a traditional hot rod should be powered by a Ford engine—either an early-era flathead four, or the more popular flathead V-8. (Non-Ford engine swaps are acceptable if executed in a "traditional" fashion.)

These are the rules as dictated by the purists. But since we're talking about hot rods, we owe it to ourselves to abide by the number one rule of rodding, which is: In hot rodding, there are no rules.

A catch-22 or a contradiction? Not really, because for the most part this book will emphasize three models of Fords—the Model T, Model A and Model B—with a chapter devoted to later-year Fords that are considered part of the original "traditional" movement. Furthermore, we won't restrict our attention to Ford-only powertrains. Some of the feature cars might have non-Ford engines, transmissions, even rear ends. Many of these hybrids are powered by Chevrolet small-block V-8s which, ironically, is the motor that displaced the Ford flattie V-8 as hot rodding's favorite engine.

But throughout this book one thing remains constant about the hot rods featured on these pages. All of the cars were either originally built 40 to 50 years ago or they were recently constructed basing their styling cues on traditional hot rods. Consequently, from curbside every hot rod in this book maintains an appearance that you could have seen on the streets or at a dry lakes meet back in the mid-forties or early fifties. It's a styling treatment that is, indeed, timeless.

Some enthusiasts, however, will argue that the traditional look is more than a timeless style. They contend the traditional look is matchless. Because, for them, nothing is finer than a traditional Ford hot rod. Those enthusiasts also will be the first to say with conviction: "Ford hot rods are forever!"

The 1997 show celebrated the L.A. Roadsters' 40th anniversary as a club. The '97 show happened to be the event's 33rd edition. Other than a brief hiatus near the beginning, the show and swap meet has been held every Father's Day weekend since 1960.

CHAPTER 1

Model T: 1908–1927

PLENTIFUL, AFFORDABLE, MODIFIABLE, RACEABLE

t's safe to say that the Model T Ford is the landmark car of the twentieth century. No other car not Volkswagen's "Beetle" nor any Chevrolet, made a more profound impact on the motoring public than the Model T managed during its 19-year production run.

It wasn't by accident that the Model T became the Industrial Revolution's automotive sensation. Henry Ford had decided from the get-go to build a car for the masses. Practically from the moment that Henry Ford regained control as major stockholder of the Ford Motor Company in 1906, he decided the Model T would be a car that could tap into the low-price market. It was a market segment that, at the time, was pretty much neglected by the auto industry. Henry Ford described the new Model T as a "universal car."

Despite its show-quality finish, Bill Nielsen's modified T resembles those built during the thirties. The body is based on the front section of a 1927 Ford touring, the four-cylinder engine from a Model A. Retro features include a reproduction Winfield head and a custom-made frame. The 16-inch, Kelsey-Hayes wheels are indicative of the period too.

A driver's-eye view lets you appreciate how the modified roadsters were able to cheat the wind. This 1927 T was narrowed 8 inches.

Prior to 1908, when the first Model T rolled off the Ford Motor Company assembly line, America and the rest of the world stubbornly clung to the past, with one foot still in the stirrups of the Horse Age. The Model T helped us out of the saddle, so that we could take the all-important second step into a new era that included machines to assist us in our everyday work and recreation.

You can thank Henry Ford, more than anybody else, for that step into the machine age. Because it was Henry Ford himself who determined that the new car should be simple in design. He also decided to make it lightweight, make it reliable, and perhaps most important of all, to make it affordable. Had there been a crystal ball on Ford's desk, he probably could have added, "And we'll make a lot of them."

History proves that Ford did exactly that. According to records, exactly 15,007,003 Model T Fords were built. It turned the aspiring Dearborn, Michigan-based automobile company into the industrial giant that it remains today.

To truly appreciate the Model T's impact on the auto industry 90 years ago, keep in mind that from 1903 to 1907 Ford had already bombarded the public with a sequence of "letter series" cars. Most of the Fords built during the early years—from the original Model A to the Model S—had sold well. Within four years after incorporating in 1903, the Ford Motor Company had established itself as an industry leader. The Model T reaffirmed the public's confidence in the Ford Motor Company.

Another way to visualize the Model T's influence on American society is to look back at the country's population during that time. By the turn of the century the census indicated slightly more than 76 million people living in the United States. That figure grew to 92 million by 1910, two years after the Model T was launched. And by 1927—the Model T's final year of production—the census figure had swelled another 30 million. When you factor in 15 million Model T Fords to the equation, you realize the popularity that the car enjoyed with the American public and the effect it had on the economy.

But beyond its impact on the general buying public and the U.S. economy, the Model T also had a major influence on the growth of the hot rod industry, which was in its infancy by 1920. That's because the Model T's availability worked in favor of early-day hot rodders and racers who, even like many of today's racers and rodders, made a habit of keeping one eye on the pocketbook whenever they modified their cars.

Within a few years of the Model T's introduction, racers realized the economic potential the car had to offer. Foremost, the Model T was affordable. And once speed-equipment manufacturers began

Chris Fuller set out to build this 1927 highboy roadster more than 20 years ago, when he was 11 years old. It's authentic early-Ford, right down to the 1932 frame, steel body, shortened 1932 grille shell, and 1940 Ford rear end with Halibrand quick-change center. The flathead V-8 has Edelbrock heads and manifold, and genuine cast-iron Fenton headers.

Dennis Love's 1927 looks just as tasty parked on the side of a country road. The car was built for less than $8,000.

developing low-priced aftermarket components for the Model T, that availability spilled over to the race track, where Model T racers were able to compete against more expensive, and more exotic, racing equipment of that era.

Consequently, the racing activity opened the door for a new aftermarket parts industry geared especially for the Model T. Within a few years names like Frontenac, Roof, Winfield, Riley, and Rajo could be found inscribed on high-performance parts destined for "Tin Lizzie" race engines. The conversion parts manifest for the 176-cubic-inch flathead engine—producing a whopping 20 horsepower in stock form at its zenith in 1927—included overhead-valve and dual-overhead-cam (DOHC) heads, high-compression flatheads, multi-lift valvetrains, even big-spark magneto ignitions. Inside the motors lurked hi-po parts, too. The manifest included high-lift camshafts, pressurized lubrication systems, and stronger clutches.

Stronger connecting rods that improved lower-end lubrication were offered, as were counter-balanced, five-bearing crankshafts. The Ruckstell Manufacturing Company even made a two-speed axle to improve the Model T's acceleration and top speed.

Most of the early "speedware" was produced in the Midwest, including parts from Rajo—an acronym that combined the first letter of Racine (Wisconsin, where the parts were built) and Joe (Jagersburger, the man who made the parts)—and Frontenac (ironically, a company formed by two of the Chevrolet brothers, Louis and Arthur; the company was based in Indianapolis). Perhaps two of the more familiar names of aftermarket parts suppliers from the West Coast were George Riley, who produced some of the more efficient cylinder heads and valve assemblies for the Model T four-cylinder engine, and Ed Winfield, a man who developed many exotic camshafts and intake systems for the venerable motor.

Howard Holman bought this modified-T roadster for several thousand dollars in 1990, then he spent several months and a few more bucks restoring it. The suicide front end was common on modified roadsters. Unlike early modified roadsters that usually were powered by Ford fours, Howard's bobtail T has a late-model Pontiac four-banger engine.

More than not, dirt-track racers in the fifties viewed C.O. Roussel's 1925 Model T from this angle. The powertrain is authentic roundy-round (slang for circle-track racing) too: a Model B Riley four-port motor, in-and-out transmission, and Warren quick-change with locked rear axle.

Even though the Model T's in-line four-cylinder engine was simple and crude by today's standards, it formed the basis for some interesting hop-up items. An obvious place to improve performance was the L-head. One popular overhead-valve conversion was the Laurel Type B, which used 16 valves—four valves per cylinder—to improve the Model T's breathing. Actually, the Laurel head was intended for touring applications. According to the company's advertisement, the Laurel Type B was "the last word in power, smoothness in operation, hill climbing ability, economy and general all around efficiency."

Other cylinder head conversions were offered by Frontenac, which included an overhead-valve (OHV) design by C. W. Van Ranst (the man who also was responsible for the development of the front-wheel-drive Cord and Packard). One of the more sophisticated designs was Robert Roof's 16-valve OHV head that was based and marketed in 1918 as "Peugeot Type Cylinder Heads for Fords."

Aftermarket carburetor kits were offered by Zenith and Ed Winfield, among others. Zenith developed a multiple-carb system that adapted to several of the high-performance cylinder head conversions, and Ed Winfield was noted for his popular Model S downdraft carburetor for the Model T. These and other hot rod conversions helped make the Model T popular both on and off the race track.

By 1923 the racing success of the Model T led to the Barber-Warnock entry in the Indianapolis 500. This car, sporting a specially made "speedster" body that was offered by one of many coach builders in the Midwest, wasn't a typical Model T. But it was, nonetheless, at heart a Ford Model T.

The Barber-Warnock racing engine was equipped with a Frontenac SR overhead-valve conversion with a Winfield carburetor. The car was driven to a fifth-place finish by L. L. Corum. Ahead of the Model T-based speedster was a quartet of Millers, considered one of the premier purpose-built race cars of that era. Not bad company for a production-based car that cost less than $300 off the showroom floor!

Despite the success of the Barber-Warnock Indy car, this and other Ford entries are overshadowed in history by the factory-Ford effort of 1935 that showcased the new flathead V-8 in a Miller-based chassis. Four team cars were entered for the prestigious race, with Ted Horn, who completed 148 laps, placing 14th in the race, highest among the Ford-Millers. (In 1933 Ford dealer C. O. Warnock entered his own V-8-based special, but it failed to qualify. The following year the car, revamped and entered as the Detroit Gasket Special, finally qualified for the 500 — with the third-slowest time. Ironically, the Detroit Gasket Special blew an engine gasket, and the entry was credited with 110 laps. A second Ford V-8-powered entry in the 1934 race was the Bohnalite Special. It launched over the wall and into obscurity on the 11th lap of the race, without serious injury to driver Chet Miller or his mechanic, Eddie Tynan.

Beyond its racing endeavors, the Model T became a mainstay among hot rodders based on two key factors: price and availability. In its first year of production the Model T sold for $550, a bargain at

A popular fiberglass replica Model T bucket was offered by Cal Automotive in the sixties. Several years ago Ron Bertrum was fortunate to locate a basket kit with this body. He restored the T-bucket, and then dropped in a 243-cubic-inch flathead V-8 for power.

Most early flathead V-8 intake manifolds housed a pair of two-barrel carbs. Another popular treatment was the tri-power, or three carb design. This particular four pot—meaning that it holds four carburetors—Edelbrock is evidence that hot rodders have always believed that more is, indeed, better.

the time. By 1924, the height of Model T production, a customer could walk into a dealership with $290, and drive out with a brand new, all-black Model T runabout roadster.

To truly appreciate the Model T's impact on the U.S. populace, it's worth comparing the car-to-population ratio in 1902, when the American automotive industry was in its infancy, with 1909, one year into the Model T's 19-year production run. According to 1902 automotive records, there was one car for every 1.5 million people in America. Within two years the ratio had shrunk to one car for every 65,000 people.

This tremendous growth led *The Nation* newspaper to predict in 1907, "As soon as a standard cheap car can be produced . . . that does not require mechan-

ical aptitude in the operation and that can be run inexpensively, there will be no limit to the automobile market." On March 19, 1908, the public was exposed for the first time to the Model T Ford. And, thanks in large part to the affordable Model T, the ratio of cars to people in 1909 had diminished to one car for every 800 people.

Despite the extraordinary number of Model Ts built, the car was not considered a technological leap forward based on auto industry standards of the time. In fact, the Model T was considered somewhat a comical piece of machinery by many Americans, which accounted for the little Ford's many nicknames, among them "Tin Lizzie" and "Flivver." Fact is, the Model T was the focal point of more than a few jokes during its reign as top-selling car in the world.

One popular witticism went like this:

"What does the Model T use for shock absorbers?"

"The passengers."

After about 10 years of production, even Ford dealers realized the Model T was trailing the rest of the automobile industry in terms of on-road performance and comfort. They begged Henry Ford, who ran his company with authoritarian rule, for a replacement car. Ford, who loved the Model T as he would his own child, responded coolly, "The only trouble with the Ford car is that we can't make them fast enough." (Henry Ford's original goal was to manufacture one Model T every minute; by 1925 the factory was rolling one out the door every 10 seconds!)

And so production continued at the Highland Park facility in Michigan. Despite the Model T's agrarian design, it accounted for 57 percent of all cars sold in the country during 1923. But by 1925 Ford sales were down to 45 percent of the market. Finally realizing that the Model T had outlived its usefulness (in terms of sales), on May 4, 1927, Henry Ford reluctantly announced to the world that his beloved car would conclude its life after the model year; a replacement would be offered for 1928. A few weeks later, May 26, Model T number 15,000,000 rolled off the assembly line.

Years after the Model T production had ceased, Henry Ford was said to have told an associate, "The only thing wrong with that car was that people stopped buying it."

But Ford was wrong. Long after the Ford Motor Company ceased production of the Model T, hot rodders began buying used Tin Lizzies by the thousands. In used condition the cars were

The heartbeat of C.O. "Rosie" Roussel's track-T racer is this Model B Ford four with Riley four-port conversion. This motor remained popular for racing until the time of the overhead-valve V-8s of the fifties.

Frank Mack built this 1926 lowboy in 1950. The car was well known throughout the Midwest, and it won Best Hot Rod at the 1953 Detroit Autorama. Mack built the entire car himself, even forming the belly pan. The motor is a modified Mercury flathead V-8.

extremely cheap, offering a young man an affordable set of wheels. Some used Model Ts in the 1930s were practically given away, selling for only a few dollars. With the variety of high-performance parts produced for racing during the previous decade, the Model T made a very attractive starting point for someone interested in building a hot rod.

The Model T remained so popular among hot rodders and nonhot rodders alike that even as late as 1949 more than 200,000 were still registered and on the highways of America. Its popularity carried

through to the 1960s, when hot rodding matured into the hobby that it is today. This popularity spawned a market for replica Model T bodies made of fiberglass. The glass bodies offered the same compact, shapely design of an original Tin Lizzie roadster body, but the builder didn't have to worry about repairing corroded metal body panels or plugging bullet holes (many abandoned Model T bodies were found in fields where the Flivver was used for target practice). One of the first aftermarket, fiberglass bodymakers was Cal Automotive, which produced a replica of the 1923 roadster, complete with turtleback deck and trunk lid.

When the hot rod mail-order boom of the mid-seventies began, the industry once again was rife with Model T aftermarket parts. Today companies such as Total Performance in Wallingford, Connecticut, and Cal Custom Roadsters in Anaheim, California, offer parts and complete Model T kit cars to the hot rod public.

Most modern fiberglass replica Model T bodies are based on the 1923 roadster. These fiberglass bodies are generally two-piece kits that have either the turtleback or a shortened pickup-bed rear section. They are commonly used for building nostalgia T-buckets and Fad Ts that were so prevalent in the seventies. Replica bodies based on the 1926–27 Model T roadster bodies are one-piece turtleback only. Generally the 1926–27 is considered to be more modern in appearance than the earlier Model Ts. Most often they are used for building Track T or highboy roadsters.

Due to the current boom in reproduction aftermarket "rodware" for the Model T, it's rather easy

In this picture, taken in 1992, the cockpit of Frank Mack's 1926 retains its original look, right down to the cracked, maroon leather upholstery, fat-faced gauges, and the huge three-spoke steering wheel. Hot rod collector Bruce Myer recently bought and restored the Mack roadster, maintaining its original charm in the process.

to build a complete car using original and mail-order components. Many of the traditional-style Model T hot rods are based on the T-bucket "Kookie Kar" concept that rod-builder Norm Grabowski conceived 40 years ago for the television series *77 Sunset Strip*. But rather than using supercharged big-block engines that sprouted on the Fad T-buckets of the seventies, the traditional Model T-based hot rods favor early Ford motors, including the Model A and Model B four-bangers, Ford's popular flathead V-8, as well as late-model OHV four-cylinder and V-8 engines.

The remainder of the drivetrain usually is based on early Ford hardware, and the suspension is formed around Model A transverse buggy springs,

or custom-fitted coil-over shock absorbers. Solid brass Model T radiator shells are acceptable, but most traditionalists today prefer to use a cut-down grille and radiator shell from a '32 Ford. And while the sophisticated four-bar linkage is more practical for aligning the front and rear axles, die-hard rodders usually insist on hairpin radius rods or split wishbones for their cars.

In any case, practically all of the traditional-style Model T hot rods today evoke the spirit of the car that prompted the aftermarket movement so many years ago. Even though hot rodding wasn't Henry Ford's original intent for the Model T, there's no disputing that his Tin Lizzie has become an integral part of the traditional hot rod movement today.

A popular update was to slip a Model A or Model B four-cylinder in front of a Model T body. This modified roadster carries a Model A engine with Winfield head and carbs. The body is a narrowed 1927 touring.

Gabby Garrison built this 1925 Model T based on one he owned in 1933 when he went to Long Beach Poly High School. The roadster has been lowered front and back. Nineteen-inch Buffalo wire wheels replace the stock wood-spoke wheels. The windshield is cut and slanted. "We called them Fords, not Model Ts, back then," said Gabby, "and hot rods were soup jobs."

Streamlining? Well, yeah, sort of. Wing nuts allow this shortened windshield to fold back. It can also be folded completely forward "so the wind could hit our faces," according to owner Gabby Garrison who built his first Model T hot rod in 1933.

Home Brew Tub

It's because of guys like Steve Wickert that hot rods evolved in the first place. Working on a tight budget, Wickert built his hot rod for less than what some collectors today would pay for an authentic set of Eddie Meyer heads and manifold. Wickert, who lives in Prescott Valley, Arizona, started the project in 1995, accumulating parts for a car that he didn't own yet.

"I was going to build a Chevy-powered hot rod," Wickert said, however, after attending the 1995 Antique Nationals, he changed his mind. "I saw how much fun they [the participants] were having, so I sold the Chevy stuff and bought the V-8-60."

Wickert happens to be handy in the machine shop, so to cut costs he whittled and shaved and filed the V8-60 block and

Steve Wickert's two-door phantom phaeton started out as a four-door sedan. It ended up as a cool hot rod.

Shown here at the 1997 Antique Nationals, Steve Wickert's $1,200 hot rod launches off the line at Los Angeles County Raceway for a 20-second pass.

heads himself until the engine was like new. To boost performance, he ported and relieved the old L-head block, and milled the heads for more compression. He also gave the little motor a 3/4-race camshaft, and stacked a single Stromberg 97 carburetor on a stock manifold. He fabricated the exhaust pipes himself, forming the steel tubing into the same relative shape as legendary Fenton exhaust headers. Finally he painted the engine red, using aerosol spray paint from the local auto parts store. The remainder of the hot rod's drivetrain is old-timie Ford running gear.

In the meantime, he kept his eyes open for a cheap buy on an old Ford body and frame. He located a shot-up Model A four-door sedan that was abandoned in the desert. Once he retrieved the sedan, he decided to chop off the top and convert the body into an open-top phaeton.

"I sawed off the top, then filled in the rear doors," Wickert said. He plugged the bullet holes and when viewed from curb-side the old sheet metal doesn't look too shabby. "If you look from the inside," Wickert confides, "you can still see where the bullet holes were."

After patching the body he put new sheet metal in the floors, ran a strip of padding around the top edge where the sedan's window garnish molding used to be, then coated the semi-straight body with red primer. Once the car was running, he set off for Palmdale, California, home of the Antique Nationals, in search of fun and good times. Wickert said that the project set him back $1,200, start to finish.

Speaking of finish, the car isn't a slouch at the drags. It posted low-20-second ETs through the quarter-mile at Los Angeles County Raceway. Not bad for a tiny flattie that breathes through a solitary Stromberg 97.

But low ETs or a low price tag isn't what this hot rod is all about. Instead, what sets Steve's hot rod apart from most others is that it represents the spirit of hot rodding as it was so many years ago.

CHAPTER 2

Model A:
1928–1931

TIMELESS
STYLE, ENDLESS
POSSIBILITIES

While the Model T was introduced to the American public at the most opportune time, Ford's timing with the Model A couldn't have come at a worse moment in automotive history. For the Tin Lizzie's replacement not only had some big shoes to fill—up to the bitter end the Model T maintained respectable sales figures—it faced stiff competition among other auto manufacturers who had, by 1928, gained a strong foothold in a market that for more than a decade was dominated by the Ford Motor Company.

By 1928 two other automobile companies emerged as FoMoCo's primary antagonists in the battle for sales supremacy. Leading the assault was General Motors, makers of the low-cost Chevrolet

Another A-V8 that Tom Leonardo Sr. managed to rescue and put back on the streets is this 1929, originally built in 1940 by the late Herman LeHam. The car is a treasure trove of prewar hot rod craftsmanship. Its mechanicals include a 1939 gearbox and rear end, Ford hydraulic brakes, split wishbones, and 16-inch, Kelsey-Hayes wheels with wide whitewall tires. The more rounded '32 Ford grille shell has always been a popular addition to Model A hot rods.

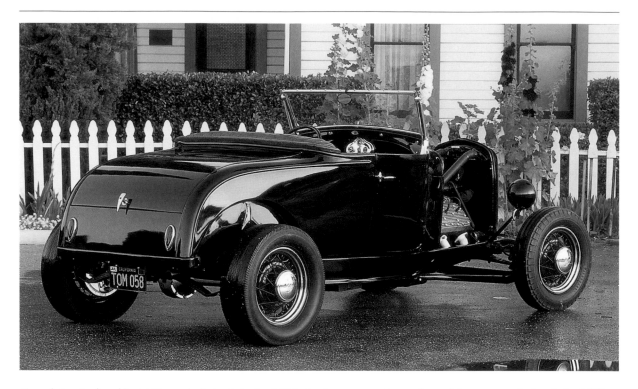

Speculation is that this A-V8 was built back in the 1950s by former moto-journalist and famous camshaft grinder William "Racer" Brown. After acquiring it in 1990, Tom Leonardo Sr. freshened it up, while maintaining the original parts. Most of all, Leonardo got the roadster running and back on the road, "where it belongs," he added.

line. GM and Ford were joined in 1925 by a relative newcomer, Chrysler Corporation. In fact, by 1927 Chevrolet had, for the first time ever, surpassed Ford in sales. Fuel was added to the fire in 1928 when the upstart Chrysler Corporation introduced its Plymouth line, giving the low-price market three strong players. Ford reluctantly moved into a two-front sales war.

Ford readied for corporate combat in two ways. First, it shifted its production to the new River Rouge plant, a huge facility where raw materials were fed in one end of the factory, and a complete car rolled out the other side. The River Rouge plant's main purpose was to produce the new Model A. Powered by an all-new four-cylinder engine, the Model A moved to the sales front October 21, 1927.

Tradition continues to roll, this time using Firestone 5.60-16 sprint car tires mounted on bent-spoke Kelsey-Hayes wire wheels. Although the rib-tread tires often were referred to as "farm implement" tires, they were actually developed for sprint car racing.

Being the first new-model Ford introduced in nearly 20 years, the Model A sparked immediate interest among the U.S. motoring public. Within 36 hours of its introduction, 10 million people nationwide had stopped by Ford dealerships to inspect Henry's new baby. In New York City alone, Ford dealers accepted cash deposits from 50,000 eager customers ready and willing to sample the new car.

The novelty quickly wore off however; shortly after the Model A debuted, Chevrolet announced that a six-cylinder engine was in the offing for its low-cost model line. This news, of course, detracted from the Model A's initial sales, and by the 1929 model year Chevrolet had gained more than a 20 percent share of a market that totaled 5,294,000 cars. Ford had, nonetheless, regained control of the sales war—about 34 percent of the market—with 1,851,000 units sold. As events unfolded, however, that situation would change. (In any case the Ford family, which privately owned the auto company in those years, could have survived even a more drastic reduction in sales. The family fortune in 1926 was estimated to be $1.2 billion—all a result of the Model T's resounding success.)

Few rodders are more enthusiastic than Jim Richardson, shown here taking his 1929 roadster for a spin. The little runabout has a Model B engine with Cragar OHV conversion, and "all the authentic stuff inside to give it more than the original 50 horsepower!" said Jim. The remainder of the drivetrain includes a Model B transmission with Zephyr 26-tooth gears and a Halibrand quick-change rear end.

For a living, Mike Armstrong grows olives on his farm in Porterville, California. And for fun, Mike drives around in this 1931 A-bone coupe that has a Model B engine with Cragar overhead conversion. The 212-cubic-inch displacement engine is fed by a pair of Stromberg 81 carbs. The 1932 transmission has 1939 gears, and the rear end is a 4.11-ratio two-speed Columbia.

But Chevrolet's six-cylinder engine was only one obstacle that the Model A had to overcome in the sales market. Economic disaster loomed over the horizon for the entire industrial world when the stock market collapsed October 29, 1929. Black Tuesday, as that catastrophic day was called, marked the beginning of an economic depression that would last throughout the subsequent decade. With the economic depression came a reduction in the number of potential new-car customers, and by the end of 1933 total new-car sales in the nation peaked at only 1,848,000. During the initial four years of the Great Depression one out of three auto makers had dropped along the wayside, and with them many of the parts vendors who kept the industry's assembly lines stocked with parts.

These economic conditions, of course, were not foreseen by Henry Ford and his son, Edsel, who had been named president of the company by his father about the time the Model T abdicated as the FoMoCo's bread-and-butter winner. As chairman of the board, Henry Ford still influenced company policy, but to his credit he allowed Edsel to oversee the design of the Model A.

Fortunately for the Model A project, Edsel was a man who appreciated art and high fashion. Consequently, when he and the Ford stylists took pencil to paper to design the Model A's sheet metal and interior, they did so with a newfound conviction to produce a car that would, once and for all, shed the plain-Jane, even agrarian, reputation that the Model T had harnessed onto the Ford Motor Company's name. Consequently, while the Model T looked square and stodgy, the Model A—for the first time in Ford's history — came across as a svelte,

Above and Right
Manny Betes built his A-V8 "back in '38 or '39, I can't really remember," he said. In any case, he and his brother, Frank, raced the car—it's little four-cylinder engine bolstered by a Riley four-port conversion—at Muroc (1941) and Rosamond (1942) dry lakes. Manny went the fastest at 107.52 miles per hour. The car is, for the most part, all original, right down to the black lacquer paint!

even stylish, automobile. Gone was any resemblance to a horse-drawn buggy. What rolled off the River Rouge assembly line was a car that looked like, well, a car!

Shortly after the Model A debuted, Henry Ford commented to the press that if there was one thing his son, Edsel, understood, it was style. As proof, he turned everybody's attention to the new Model A. The buying public obviously agreed, as the Model A accounted for more than five million sales during its four-year life span.

Foremost, the Model A lacked the "spindly" appearance of the Model T. The new car sprouted stylish bumpers and contoured running board aprons for a more refined appearance. Furthermore, its larger, more curvaceous body was adorned by wider, yet sleeker, fenders. Its appearance was more up-scale, too, thanks to the chromed radiator shell.

The Model A's interior broke new ground for FoMoCo cars, too. Biggest news of all was the spacious seating for driver and occupants, a treatment that was inherited from Ford's acquisition of the

Lincoln line of luxury cars. The new Model A also had a floor-mounted hand-shifter to operate the new three-speed transmission, and a more thorough array of instruments were positioned in the center of the dashboard. Topping off the interior was a new 21-inch diameter steering wheel that was in sharp contrast to the Model T's inverted wheel, a carryover from the automobile industry's infancy.

Interestingly, the designation Model A broke tradition with Ford's policy for naming new models. From the first Ford through the Model T, each subsequent model name had been determined by the next letter in the alphabet; thus, Model B followed the original Model A, C followed B, and so forth. By rights, the 1928 Model A should have been termed the Model U, however, Henry Ford was so taken by the demise of his beloved Model T, and he harbored such high hopes that its successor would breathe new life into the auto company, that he christened Edsel's car after FoMoCo's first automobile, built near the turn of the century. And so, Model A it was. This turn around also was a tribute to Edsel in certain ways, marking the beginning of what appeared to be a new era for the largest automobile company in the world.

Not only did the Model A boast new styling and a more spacious interior, its drivetrain was new and improved over the Model T's. The planetary-gear transmission was replaced by a three-speed transmission with a floor-mounted shifter. The Model A's frame, although based on a pair of parallel straight rails on either side similar to that found on the Model T, was larger and stronger. Most of all, the Model A's engine, although still an in-line four-cylinder like the T's, boasted more displacement and more power.

Henry Ford and engineer Lawrence S. Sheldrick were instrumental in the new engine's design. This turned out to be good and bad news, though, because while Sheldrick offered some interesting design concepts that eventually led to improved power, it was Henry Ford's continued affection for the Model T that, in all probability, meant that the Model A engine unnecessarily shared more similarities than dissimilarities with its predecessor.

Regardless, the Model A's engine was bigger than the Model T's. Displacement was 200.5 cubic inches compared to 176.7 cubic inches. The A's bore and stroke was 3.875x4.250 inches versus the T's 3.750x4.000 inches. Even so, initial dynamometer

Above and Right
Other than the key fob, the interior on Manny's 1929 roadster is original. Remember, this is a 60-year-old car. In contrast, the interior to Joe Scanlin's 1929 boasts all-new vinyl, although the Auburn dash and four-spoke roadster steering wheel are indicative of what rodders did to their cars in the early days.

tests indicated that the new A motor produced no more horsepower than the T. Both peaked at 20 horsepower! Obviously, this wasn't satisfactory, and with only a few weeks before the new car bowed to the U.S. public, Henry Ford sent Sheldrick and his engineering team back to the engine room with a decree —double the horsepower.

Records show that Sheldrick had about three weeks to perform the miracle. Despite the short period of time, he came through with flying colors. The first Model A four-bangers developed 40 horsepower. The remedy centered around enlarged water passages for more efficient cooling. That taken care of, Sheldrick's team was able to improve intake breathing by fitting a Y-type intake manifold with a Zenith carburetor, and matching the engine's gas-

kets to their respective port-tunnel openings. Doubling the engine's horsepower didn't affect its reliability, either; the Model A had 1.500-inch rod bearings and 1.625-inch main bearings as opposed to the Model T's 1.250-inch bearings (rod and main).

Despite doubling its horsepower, the Model A was vastly underpowered compared to the competition. By comparison, the Chrysler's six-cylinder model produced 54 horsepower, and Buick advertised 63 horsepower for its big motor. Even Chrysler's new Plymouth, which debuted the same year as the Model A, had a four-cylinder engine that produced 45 horsepower, good for a 60 mile-per-hour top speed.

The new low-cost ($670) Plymouth also featured a hydraulic brake system. Henry Ford steadfastly refused to acknowledge the benefits of hydraulic brakes for cars, and so the Model A, like the Model T, had mechanically operated brake shoes, which required more pedal pressure by the driver in order to stop the car.

Of course, hot rodders then, as in years to come, weren't necessarily concerned with the Model A's stopping ability. Instead, their interest in Ford's new car was in how *fast* it could go, especially on the southern California dry lake beds where organizations such as the Muroc Racing Association began promoting speed events as early as March 25, 1931, when the Gilmore Oil Company sponsored an organized meet on the famous dry lake bed. And through this quest for speed the Model A race enthusiasts spawned a whole new movement among the performance parts builders.

Two of the leading parts suppliers were George Riley and Ed Winfield. As they had done with the Model T, Riley was known for his Model A overhead-valve conversions, while Winfield made a name for himself offering camshafts and carburetors for the new Ford.

Perhaps Riley's two most noteworthy contributions to the new Ford four-cylinder engines were the two-port and four-port heads. The two-port head was the earlier design, utilizing a pair of Siamese intake tunnels leading from a tubular intake manifold. The new cylinder head had two intake overhead valves per cylinder, while the stock L-block (or flathead) exhaust valves remained in operation within the engine's cylinder block. The two-port conversion was so successful at speed

Fords built before 1939 did not have hydraulic brakes. When Ford equipped its cars with "juice" brakes in 1939, the hot rodders were quick to follow. This 1929 Ford with 1932 grille has brakes from a 1940 Ford.

events that George Riley later published a booklet titled *Building the 100 m.p.h. Model A Ford* (recently reprinted by old-Ford aficionado Dan Iandola), and a brief article, "Secrets of Speed."

In his article about performance tuning the Model A, Riley wrote, "In building fast Ford speedsters and racers (and if you don't think some of the western cars are fast, ask eastern boys who have raced here), it has always been our endeavor to change standard Ford construction no more than absolutely necessary. This gives the Ford racing car the advantage of being able to obtain parts and service anywhere." In short, Riley paid tribute to the Model A's adaptability as a hot rod engine. It's simplicity and resounding

durability ensured it to be a solid candidate for building a hot rod or racer. And, by limiting the modifications to its original design, the hot rod conversion could be performed for relatively few dollars.

Riley offered an economical performance Model A cylinder head, too. It was a bolt-on flathead, offering 5.8:1 compression ratio from its 13/16-inch depth combustion chambers. The Riley flathead, which sold for $21.50 in 1930, had a combustion chamber design that was "buldged [*sic*] or curved to provide additional clearance around valves and yet the cylinder head covers a standard Ford head gasket," according to a Riley advertisement in 1931. In essence, the spark plugs were located in the center of the combustion chamber for a more uniform flame front. The result was "unquestionably the most powerful and smoothest performing flat head available for the Model A Ford motor," so said Riley's advertisement.

Unquestionably, though, it was the two-port design that a large number of Model A hot rodders sought. Three distinct Riley two-port head configurations were produced. The Model B was intended for highway use, while the Model C was for racing purposes only. Riley also offered a Model D, which was best suited for "trucks having 70 horsepower engines, with same load." (Don't confuse Riley's Model B or Model C conversions with Ford's 1932 Model B or 1933 Model C four cylinders.)

Riley advertisements of the era boasted an 80-mile-per-hour performance for an otherwise stock Model A Ford equipped with the Model B Riley two-port head. The Model C Riley head boasted more compression and more top speed (this was the cylinder head that was the topic of discussion in his 100-mile-per-hour Model A Ford booklet). All three heads shared similar combustion chamber designs; the two intake valves were positioned almost directly over the combustion chamber, while an adjoining pocket atop the L-block's exhaust valve housed the spark plug. The flame front was initiated here, according to Riley's records, to avoid pre-ignition of unburned gases as they began to exit through the exhaust port.

Perhaps the most unique feature about the Riley head is the double-forked rocker-arm mechanism that operates the two intake valves. These rocker-arm assemblies are shrouded by a pair of valve covers that resemble inverted cooking pots. The name "Riley

Steve Wickert performed much of his own engine work on this flathead. The V-8-60 has milled heads, a modified engine block, 3/4 race cam, and a single Stromberg 97 on a stock manifold.

Tom Leonardo Jr. built his 1930 roadster for about $1,000. Of course, it helped that his father's garage and backyard are stocked with literally tons of genuine old Ford parts that he could use.

Racing" is inscribed on the top of each valve cover. The two-port heads have the intake and exhaust ports on the right side of the engine. The four-port can be identified because its intake is on the left side.

There were numerous other performance-parts suppliers for Ford's new Model A four-cylinder engine. Companies such as Duray, Alexander, Cragar, Gemsa, Murphy, Rutherford and Sparks, among others, offered flathead, OHV, or single- and double-overhead camshaft conversions. And hot rodders adapted updraft and downdraft carburetors from such companies as Winfield and Zenith to specially made intake manifolds.

The Model A engine also endeared itself to hot rodders because its lubrication system could be updated to Model B (Ford) specs, giving it a pressurized system. One hot rodder of the thirties, John Athan, eventually sold his Model T hot rod to a friend, stepping up to a modified Model A to rid himself of the early Ford engine's lubrication worry. Athan, who grew up in Culver City, California, one of the hot beds for early-day hot rodding, sold his car to a young man who would eventually make a name for himself in hot rodding—Ed Iskenderian.

Athan and Isky—as Iskenderian became known by his hot rod cronies—chummed around together as young hot rodders. When Athan could finally afford to buy a used Model A, he sold his Model T hot rod to Isky (who, to this day, still owns the classic 1926-based hot rod). As Athan explains the transaction, "I didn't want a Model T anymore. I wanted something with oil pressure. So I sold it [the Model T hot rod] to Ed. Then he could worry about what it [the motor] was going to do!"

Actually, when it came to absolute top speed both Athan and Isky favored Model A engines with Cragar conversions. A Cragar four-banger was good for "about

Hot rods and race cars shared much the same speedware during the prewar years. This Depression-era champ car has a Ford four-cylinder engine with a Riley four-port conversion, a similar system that hot rodders applied to their street-going cars.

120 miles per hour," at the dry lakes, said Athan, while early Ford V-8-powered hot rods could usually muster only about a 100-mile-per-hour top speed. A major reason, of course, was that prior to World War II, few people or companies made high-performance products for the new Ford V-8, while aftermarket parts for the four-bangers remained plentiful.

Given that, the situation during the prewar years remained promising for the Model A, and later Model B and Model C four-cylinder engines, because there were so *many* performance players involved. In fact, as many as a dozen manufacturers can be listed for flathead, overhead-valve (OHV), overhead-cam (OHC), or dual-overhead-cam (DOHC) conversions alone. This doesn't include ignition, carburetion, exhaust and intake manifolds, and camshaft suppliers.

Eventually, as we'll discuss in the next chapter, the popularity—and top speed—of the flathead V-8 overtook the venerable four-bangers. Even so, today hot rod enthusiasts have rediscovered the fun and excitement to be had in building a truly fast and reliable early Ford four-cylinder engine. Today, as was the case more than half a century ago, the legendary Ford Model A engine enjoys a widespread popularity among hot rod engine builders.

But while the Model A four-cylinder engine had slipped into temporary dormancy among postwar hot rodders, the 1928–31 body has always been a favorite for transforming an early Ford into a go-fast street machine. Simply, the Model A is considered one of the all-time beautiful Ford bodies and especially lends itself to customizing. In particular, rodders tend to prefer 1928 and 1929 Model A bodies, due to the elegant look afforded it by the curved character revealed down the sides of the cowl. The 1930 and 1931 bodies look similar, but are slightly more spacious than the 1928 and 1929, and lack the cowl accent lines.

When the 1932 V-8 was introduced, many racers realized the new engine's potential for speed. They also understood that the more compact Model A body punched a smaller hole in the wind than that of a '32 Ford during a top-speed pass down the dry lake. Consequently, an early fix for making a fast roadster during the dawning of the V-8 era was to mount a Model A body onto a 1932 Ford frame that already carried a 100-horsepower flathead V-8 engine. These hybrids (as well as Model A hot rods with flathead V-8s shoehorned inside the stock frame rails) were known as A-V8s among hot rodders.

Today Model A roadsters, coupes, and Tudor sedans are considered prize catches for hot rodding. There remains a wealth of genuine all-steel bodies, but several companies offer brandnew replica bodies as well. Brookville Roadsters makes an all-steel reproduction roadster body, while Downs, Gibbon, and Wescott's are known for their fiberglass reprobodies in roadster and coupe configurations.

Best of all, though, a large number of original Model A hot rods that were built shortly before or after World War II—the hey-day of hot rodding according to many traditionalists—have survived the years, and can be seen on the road or at rod runs to this day. Many of these Model A hot rods have become recognized for what they are, rolling museum pieces that tell us exactly what hot rodding was like in the days before overhead-valve V-8 engines became the norm from Detroit. It was a halcyon time when hot rodders built four-cylinder engines that could punch 120-mile-an-hour holes in the wind, or punch a hole through the crankcase trying. Legends were made during those days, and other young men drifted into obscurity while chasing their dreams. Regardless, anybody who has ever owned a Model A hot rod will agree that this Ford is one of the most beloved styles offered by Henry Ford's company.

Antique Nationals

A favorite drag race meet among traditional-style hot rod enthusiasts is the Antique Nationals, but people attending the Antique Nats—held every year during the first weekend of June at Los Angeles County Raceway near Palmdale, California —shouldn't expect ground-rumbling diggers to numb their senses with smoking-tire runs down the quarter-mile. Remember, we're talking about antique cars here. According to the event flyer the meet is open to "only 1954 and earlier type vehicles, any engine, stock to race cars."

The event attracts a wide variety of antique cars, too. Beyond the restored oldies that show up, a bulk of the participants include early-style hot rods and former race cars, even oval-track dirt racers. Due to the wide range of pre-1955 entries, the Antique Nats have become a favorite event for people who love traditional-style hot rods.

To maintain parity among the drag racers, the event format is based on typical bracket racing, so everybody stands a chance of winning. At a typical meet there are about a dozen racing classes, plus Powder Puff and vintage motorcycles. Usually winners and runners-up receive trophies, plus a few donated prizes from supporting sponsors. There's also a custom car show that the promoters, the Four Ever Four Car Club, stage in the parking lot for hot rods and customs of any vintage.

But trophies—even winning—isn't the main draw that attracts the hundreds of participants to the Antique Nats. As Four Ever Four member Jim Siegmund once explained, "This is a real low-pressure, no-money (prize money) event."

A Model T runabout takes an excursion down the drag strip — and back through time for its driver and passenger.

Spectators are welcomed to stroll the pits and prestage lanes, where they can see the cars and talk to the owners. It's a relaxed atmosphere—just like the good ol' days!

Rightfully so, because most of the competitors are more concerned about the fun factor than their cars' quarter-mile top speeds and elapsed times. It's not uncommon to see a bone-stock Model T sedan power through the standing quarter-mile in under 40 seconds, or watch as two four-cylinder Model A hot rods face off for a sub-20-second blast!

In any case, the Antique Nats offers traditional-style hot rod enthusiasts a chance to mingle with some die-hard hot rodders, and to examine their unique cars up close. Admission to the bleachers also gets you into the pits, where the early iron and old tin sits between elimination rounds. Spectators can cruise through the pits, talk with the racers, and even take time to snoop inside the engine compartments for a close look-see at some very rare speed equipment.

The Antique Nationals isn't for everybody, nor was it meant to be. The first events were promoted back in the mid-1960s at the now-defunct Orange County International Raceway. Instead, the Antique Nationals is an event where old cars can act young again.

A couple of Model A Fords line up for the start. The racing is sort-of-fast, and sort-of-furious, and most certainly very fun.

CHAPTER 3

Dawn of the Flathead V-8: 1932

THE RODDER'S HOLY GRAIL

P ractically every hot rod aficionado on this planet is in agreement about one thing: 1932 was a landmark year for hot rodding. That's because the 1932 Ford—above all other Fords and non-Fords — is the car that has carried the hot rod banner higher than any other car. Furthermore, the 1932 Ford marked the beginning of a new chapter in Ford Motor Company history—the first Ford V-8 engine.

Few people will dispute that the 1932 Ford represents one of the most remarkable body styles ever achieved by an automobile company. As a result, the '32 Ford's legend has been etched in the pages of countless hot rod enthusiast periodicals and books. One editor for a prominent, national, hot rod magazine proclaimed: "It doesn't get any better than a Deuce highboy roadster. You have that, and

Lewis Wolff built this Deuce roadster in 1963, and it won its class at the Cobo Hall Show in Detroit that same year. It later appeared in the March 1964 issue of Hot Rod magazine. Even more remarkable, its candy apple red paint job remains intact today.

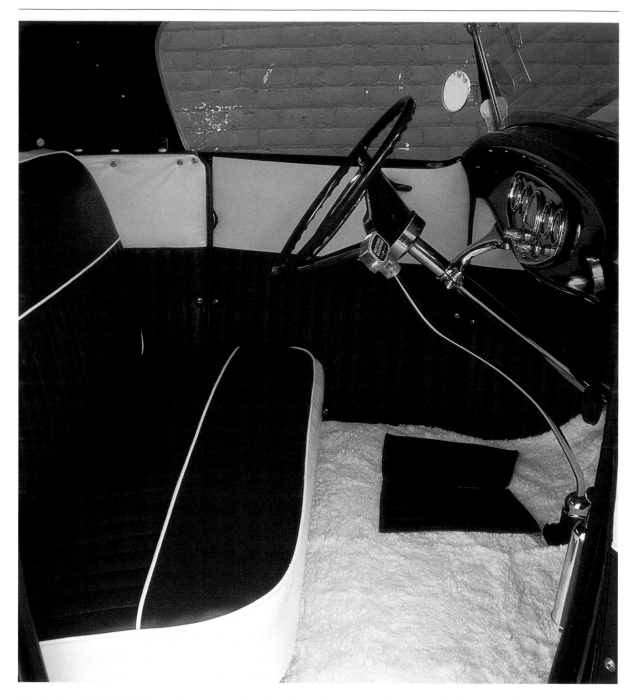

The interior of Wolff's 1932 roadster was stitched for show. The 1962 Ford steering wheel is mounted to a traditional-style column that's been chromed — for show. The white carpet and red-and-white Naugahyde upholstery look as fresh today as in 1963 when Lewis completed the car.

you're at the top of the hot rod food chain."

To appreciate his statement, you should fully understand what a Deuce highboy roadster is, and why it's so special among rodders. First, the word "Deuce." Simply, that was the name hot rodders adopted for their beloved 1932 Ford; the Deuce was in reference to the "2" of 1932. And whenever a hot rodder says "Deuce," there's no question that he's talking about a 1932 Ford. It was the only year Ford offered this particular model—sometimes referred to as the Model B.

The word "roadster" refers to a two-passenger open-top model without roll-up windows. Due to its rather compact size, and the lack of a steel top, roll-up side windows and the accompanying crank mechanisms inside the door panels, the roadster was the lightest—and least expensive—model offered. The Deuce roadster became a prime target for serious hot rodders who preferred to spend as little money as possible (they couldn't afford much anyway!) for a car that weighed as little as possible (remember, less weight translates to improved performance).

Which brings us to the key word "highboy" in our Deuce discussion. In order to shave more weight from the car for street drag racing (popular,

Joe Scanlin restored this three-window from a hot rod that originally was built in 1956 by Ray Jones. The coupe has had several different engines, including an Oldsmobile V-8 and a fuel-injected Chevy 283. Most recently its powertrain is based on traditional hardware: a 276-cubic-inch Merc flathead delivers power to a Halibrand V-8 quick-change, via a 1939 Ford transmission with 26-tooth Zephyr gears.

but highly illegal then, as now) and to improve aerodynamics for top-speed dry lakes racing, the early-day hot rodders often removed their Deuce roadster's fenders and bumpers. Due to the 1932 Ford frame's unique configuration, the fenderless hot rod assumed a high stance on its frame rails. Thus the term "highboy".

The Deuce's signature could be found in its stylishly contoured frame rails. Up to 1932 all Ford frames had been formed around a pair of simple, straight rails. The 1932 frame was different. Ford stylists, led by Gene Farkas and Edsel Ford, purposely designed the 1932 frame rails to sit directly beneath the body's lower side panels. This was a major shift from the earlier frame design for the Model T and Model A. By contrast, the Deuce's frame rails followed the bottom curve of the restyled body, eliminating the need for splash aprons, as used on the Model A. To smooth the transition between the frame rail and the running board assembly, the stylists incorporated a flared character reveal, or lip, into the bottoms of the rails. Coincidentally, when the fenders were removed for racing or rodding, it became visually obvious that the Deuce's body actu-

The Ford flathead V-8, also known as the "flattie" among rodders, was produced from 1932 through 1953. A variation of the engine included the V8-60, a 136-cubic-inch motor that was supposed to replace the Model C four-cylinder. The V8-60 got its name from the design—a V-8—and the horsepower—60. The V8-60 was only warmly received in 1937, and within four years it was shelved. It was, however, a popular motor for midget race cars of the 1940s and 1950s.

Scott DaPron started with a fully restored 1932 Ford roadster to build this replica of a car that his father and grandfather raced in the 1934 Gilmore Cup. All the parts, including the cast magnesium wheels, hood straps, and cut windshield are original old parts that Scott located at automotive swap meets.

ally perched itself atop the frame rails. Rodders quickly referred to their fenderless Deuce hot rods as highboys, and the name also applied to hot rods using Model A and Model T bodies set atop Deuce frame rails (a common practice even today).

Ford also refined the rear suspension for 1932. Previous Fords positioned the rear leaf spring above the rear axle housing. To clear the Model A third member, the buggy-style leaf spring had a pronounced arch in the center section. This set the car high in the air. To lower the body for '32, the rear spring was relocated behind the rear axle. By doing so, the leaf spring didn't require the high center arch, so the spring was flatter. By using a flatter leaf spring the engineers were able to incorporate a kick-up to the rear section of the frame, so that the body sat as low as possible to the ground. Gene Farkas, Ford's designer who played a key role in the '32's styling, used this configuration to help attain the new car's low stance. Farkas also opted for 18-inch rather than 19-inch wheels to maintain proper proportions. New-style, welded-spoke Kelsey-Hayes wheels were used. Coincidentally, these 18x3.5-inch wheels had 32 spokes.

The Model B four-banger in DaPron's roadster has authentic high-performance parts. The intake manifold is made of tubular steel and is stacked with a pair of Winfield SR downdraft carbs. Scott races the car at various nostalgia drag races. "After all," he enthusiastically said, "that's what cars are for."

Henry Ford specifically ordered the use of the old buggy-style leaf springs, once stating: "We use transverse springs for the same reason that we use round wheels, because we have found nothing better for the purpose." Henry Ford's decision, as usual, was based on the profiteer's axiom, "If it ain't broke, then don't fix it."

As the years rolled by, however, some 1932 Fords were relegated to junkyard status. Others found temporary residence in used car lots. And through time the aging Deuce became affordable for hot rodding purposes. A common practice among hot rodders of the late 1940s was to replace the rather large Deuce body with that of a Model T or Model A. Model A roadsters equipped with a flathead V-8 became known as A-V8s. By mounting a Model T or Model A roadster or coupe (and, to a lesser degree, two-door sedan) body to a '32 Ford frame, they could further reduce weight and improve aerodynamics because the older bodies were narrower. Best of all, by slipping a lighter Ford body onto the 1932 frame rails, the hot rodders could better utilize the horsepower advantage from Ford's new V-8. The body swap required several modifications. The wider cross-members of the '32 were replaced with narrower ones to match the body width of the earlier Fords. Another common practice, starting in the mid-1940s, was to adapt hydraulic brakes (first introduced by Ford in 1939) to the highboys. The hydraulic brakes improved stopping ability, especially for the V-8-powered hot rods. In hot rodder language hydraulic brakes were commonly referred to as "juice" brakes.

To be sure, the big news in 1932 throughout the automotive world was the debut of Ford's V-8 motor. The project began in secrecy in 1930, in an engine-development facility known as the Blue Room. The engineers worked feverishly on the project and within two years the Ford Motor Company accomplished what no other car company had ever achieved—they designed, developed, and put into production an affordable V-8 automobile engine.

The new Ford V-8 engine block was based on a one-piece, or monobloc, design that required only a single casting step. Previously, most other mass-produced V-8 engines—such as Cadillac, LaSalle, and Lincoln, a company that Ford acquired a few years before—were based on two- or three-piece engine blocks. Ford advertisements boasted that the new monobloc V-8 was: "An engine with worlds of power to spare that by the very brilliance of its performance, new principles of design and construction will prove to you what advanced motor design can mean." The advertisement further claimed a top speed of "75 mph in high" gear.

Logic dictates that hot rodders quickly warmed to the prospects of utilizing the 65-horsepower engine for their forays across the dry lake beds or

A pair of vintage, military aircraft seats, a four-spoke roadster wheel, a 60-year-old tachometer, and single-piece door panels— old-style hot rodding doesn't get much better than this! Note the classic Gilmore plaque on the dashboard.

through their local back-road "drag strips." That wasn't the case. Due to its relative newness, there were few V-8 aftermarket speed parts available during the pre-World War II years. Modified Ford four-cylinder engines were capable of producing more horsepower than a stock V-8, so the hot rodders remained faithful to their little fours.

When the Ford V-8 bowed in 1932, the speed merchants had developed an array of worthy and reliable performance components for the Model A four-cylinder engine. And, since the new Model B four-cylinder (standard fare for 1932) was based on the Model A design, most of the existing speed equipment readily adapted to the new Deuce four-banger as well.

The Model B four-cylinder engine was considered a better engine than its Model A predecessor. Based on horsepower output alone, the Model B was 20 percent better, producing 50 horsepower compared to the Model A's 40 horsepower. Several factors played roles in this gain, including higher lift cam lobes, increased compression ratio—4.6:1 vs. 4.2:1—and a 1.25-inch-venturi carburetor that was force-fed by a fuel pump. In addition, the Model B's lubrication system was pressurized (first time for a four-cylinder Ford), utilizing an oil pump to maintain constant oil pressure. In short, this was a hot rod engine, but one that evolved more by chance than by choice.

Oddly, it wasn't the B-motor's additional horsepower that sparked the hot rodders' interest. Instead, it was the motor's more rugged design. The new B-four had larger bearings for the crankshaft and rods (2.000-inch and 1.875-inch, respectively, vs. the Model A's bearings that measured 1.500-inches

The interior to Hartman's 1932 coupe is finished as nicely as the body. Tan leather covers the stock bench seat and the 1936 Ford banjo-style steering wheel rim. The dash is original, with classic instruments and a column-mount tachometer.

at all journals), and the crankshaft itself was counterbalanced, weighing 10 pounds more than the Model A (despite the heavier crankshaft, the Model B engine tipped the scales at 447 pounds, compared to the Model A's 473). As a precaution to make sure that the lower-end bearings received plenty of oil at sustained high engine speeds, many hot rodders drilled the cranks to improve oil pressure to the rod bearings, and they shaved off the rod dipper-buckets, because those sump scoops were no longer needed to enssure adequate oil delivery.

While the Model B four-cylinder engine showed great promise for hot rodding, it was Ford's new V-8 that captured the spotlight throughout the automotive world in general, for no other auto manufacturer had ventured into the realm that Henry Ford

was willing to enter that year. Actually, Ford enthusiasts can thank Chevrolet for Henry Ford's decision to build the new V-8; when General Motors launched its 1929 Chevrolet model with an in-line six-cylinder engine, Dearborn's number one citizen defiantly proclaimed, "We are going to go from a four to an eight, because Chevrolet is going to a six."

Prior to that, Henry Ford had steadfastly refused to build anything other than four-cylinder engines, backing that corporate policy with his famous quote: "I've got no use for a motor that has more spark plugs than a cow has teats." Abiding by his practice to lead rather than follow, however, Henry Ford instructed his engineers—as far back as 1922—to experiment with an engine concept known as X8.

The X8 engine was an interesting design that had two rows of cylinders on top and bottom, which accounted for the X8 nomenclature. The engine was compact, and even fit inside the Model T's rather restrictive engine bay. Unfortunately, the design was fraught with flaws, among them oil-fouled spark plugs in the lower, inverted combustion chambers. Excessive oil dripped into the lower cylinders, fouling the plugs. In the end, the X8 became just another ex-program in FoMoCo's storied past. Its failure to reach the production stage further solidified Henry Ford's disdain for anything other than four-cylinder engine designs. That attitude changed quickly in 1929 when Chevrolet, with its new six-cylinder, upstaged Ford in the quest to lead rather than follow.

As with the Model A four-cylinder update, Laurence Sheldrick was put in charge of the V-8 project. Sheldrick enlisted Ford engineer Arnold Soth to pen the original design. Initial test engines were based on a rather compact design with a 60-degree valley between the cylinders. This was an ill-fated motor, giving way to the 90-degree format that ultimately debuted in 1932.

Early prototypes were designated Model 24 by Ford's research and development team, and the early prototype boasted displacement of 232.5 cubic inches. By February 1931 the new engine was ready for road testing. Ultimately Blue Room engineers reduced the displacement to 221 cubic inches, based on bore and stroke dimensions of 3.062 inches and 3.750 inches, respectively.

By 1946 the Ford Motor Company had refined its V-8. This version, the fabled 59A model, powers Wayne Hartman's classic coupe. Genuine hot rod wares include Navarro heads, a tall Tattersfield dual-carb manifold with a pair of Stromberg 97s on top.

L.A. Roadsters member Bob Dyar commissioned long-time hot rodder Dick Smith to build him this 1932 highboy in 1972. Smith did all the work himself, except stitch the tan upholstery and spray on the candy magenta paint. The car was ahead of its time, boasting several hand-machined, billet aluminum pieces such as the shock shrouds and a dash-mounted fuel-pressure-pump knob. The Halibrand wheels are real magnesium (polished), and Smith fashioned the grille insert using stainless steel sections. Truly a beautiful car in 1972 and today.

Because Ford already had extensive research data and real-world experience on flathead (L-head) four-cylinder engines, the V-8 used that configuration. In an effort to conserve money on research and development, Henry Ford instructed his design team to utilize various components from the four-cylinder engine. For instance, he told the V-8 engineers to equip the new motor with existing water pumps from the Model B four-cylinder, a move that proved to be disastrous. In this case, two pumps—one for each cylinder head—were mounted at the return-side of the engine's cooling system, which meant they had to extract hot water from the engine, rather than pull cool water from the radiator. This layout proved ineffective in circulating the coolant fast enough, and the heated water had a habit of turning to steam inside the water jackets before entering the radiator for cool down. The result was a plethora of overheating engines in the early years of the flathead V-8's 22-year existence.

Despite the overheating problems, people everywhere embraced Ford's new V-8 because it had something that few affordable cars offered—power. During the early years, if someone said, "I bought a new V-8," it was understood that they were talking specifically about a Ford V-8. For its time the flathead V-8 was considered a powerful engine, developing 65 horsepower at 3,400 rpm and 30 foot-pounds of torque at 1,250 rpm.

The original V-8 had a 5.5:1 compression ratio, and the rods and pistons turned a 65-pound, forged-steel crankshaft that rode on three main

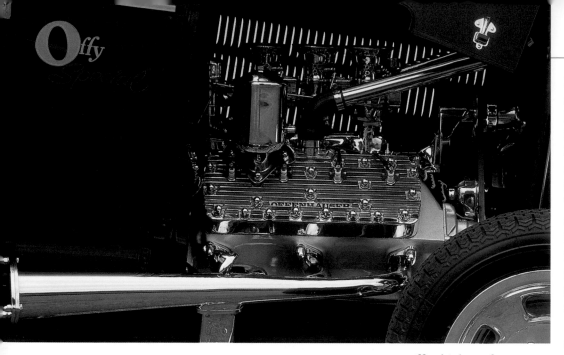

Bob Dyar's Offy Special is truly special. The 59A flattie motor has Offenhauser heads and manifold. Additional high-performance add-ons for the 284-cubic-inch V-8 include an Isky camshaft and Harmon-Collins magneto. Dick Smith formed the tube headers himself, and made the stylish hood clips, along with a host of other parts too numerous to list.

bearings. The camshaft and connecting rods were made of forged steel and the self-adjusting valves—with 1.537-inch faces—were constructed of high-chrome silicon alloy steel. Early V-8s were fed by single-throat, 1.25-inch-venturi Detroit Lubricator carbs. The original design had 21-stud heads. Later editions, beginning in late 1938, had 24-stud heads, and generally are considered to be superior motors for hot rodding purposes.

But it was the company's very first 21-stud head engine that Henry Ford personally stamped the engine ID numbers "18-1" into that turned out to be a landmark for Ford and the auto industry. For that was the first of more than 12 million flathead V-8 motors to be made by America's premier auto maker. Today engine number 18-1 is exhibited at the Ford Museum in Dearborn, Michigan.

The Ford flathead V-8 is revered as the consummate traditional-style hot rod engine today.

Literally hundreds of speed records have been established with Ford flathead V-8s, the Beach Boys rock-and-roll group immortalized the engine in their "Little Deuce Coupe" song, and countless books have been written regarding the flattie's worth as the supreme nostalgic hot rod motor.

Among the first speed merchants to offer high-performance equipment for the flattie was Vic Edelbrock Sr. Shortly after migrating from Kansas to California in 1931, Edelbrock opened an auto repair shop on Wilshire Boulevard in Beverly Hills, California. In 1934 he moved his business to the corner of Venice and Hoover in nearby Los Angeles, and about that time he bought his first car to build into a hot rod for the dry lakes. The car was a V-8-powered 1932 Ford roadster.

From the get-go Edelbrock made his Deuce roadster race-worthy for dry lakes racing. His search for more horsepower led him to Tommy Thickston, a man who designed and built Ford four-cylinder speed equipment. Thickston, with Edelbrock's help, developed an aluminum, dual-carb, intake manifold for the flathead V-8. The manifold was marketed under Thickston's name, but Edelbrock wasn't satisfied with its performance on the race track. So he set off to design and build his own manifold. The result was the Slingshot, a twin-pot manifold that used a pair of Stromberg 97 carburetors for intake. Only about 100 of the Slingshot manifolds were built before production was suspended when America entered World War II. Today original Slingshot manifolds built before the war are extremely rare and valuable among Ford flathead collectors.

But when Edelbrock—the businessman—built his first Slingshot manifold, Edelbrock — the racer —wasn't concerned about how much his cast-aluminum fixtures would be worth. Instead, young Edelbrock valued how well they propelled his roadster across the dry lake bed. And in 1941, only three weeks before the United States officially entered World War II, Edelbrock's Slingshot-equipped, Deuce highboy roadster was clocked at 121.42 miles per hour over Rosamond Dry Lake.

Edelbrock spent the duration of the war as a fabricator, making parts for the military. After the war he purchased his first building, in Hollywood, where he resumed business in the speed-equipment industry. Almost immediately Edelbrock returned to racing, this time with midget dirt-track cars. He designed and built much of his own speed equipment for Ford V-8s, including parts for the compact V8-60 that was popular among midget dirt-track racers during that era (The V8-60 was a compact version of the standard V-8, which, by 1937, produced 85 horsepower. The V8-60 was based on a similar, but smaller, engine block. Cylinder displacement was 136 cubic inches, and the "economy motor" produced 60 horsepower — thus the name V8-60. The V8-60 was introduced in 1937 and was offered for only four years. It was conceived as an economical replacement for the Model C four-cylinder that was offered only in 1933. Americans never thoroughly embraced the V8-60 concept, so Ford ceased production of the "baby" V-8 after 1940, replacing it with the first Ford in-line six-cylinder in 1941.). Edelbrock's speed-equipment business flourished, and today the company he founded offers a wide range of high-performance ware — including Ford flathead parts based on those that Vic Sr. developed more than 50 years ago.

Edelbrock wasn't the only name found stamped on speed parts for Ford's flathead V-8. Many of the vendors offering speedware for the Model A and B four-cylinder engines joined the V-8 movement, too. Reputable companies such as Winfield, Riley, Gemsa, Cragar, and Rutherford built performance parts for the new Ford V-8. Among the new names to join the list were Eddie Meyer and McDowell and Ardun. Today Edelbrock and Offenhauser offer a wide range of flathead parts for hot rodders building flathead motors. Eddie Meyer replica heads and intake manifolds are offered, too, along with Kong Jackson and Barney Navarro high-compression heads based on designs they perfected in the fifties. There also are several aftermarket camshafts, including the renowned Potvin (now by Mooneyes) and Ed Iskenderian's famous grind, plus ignition-update systems and many replacement internal parts to keep hot-rodded flathead V-8s on the road for years to come.

No doubt, in the beginning it was the V-8 engine that enamored the automotive community to the 1932 Ford, but it was the Deuce's unique body style that truly captivated hot rod enthusiasts during the ensuing years. After all, this was the Ford model that, for a welcomed change, emphasized form equally with function. True, the Model A was considered a quantum leap forward in the company's attention to body styling, but that car carried over some of the Model T's out-dated traits such as a square-sided, chrome-plated grille shell, cowl-mounted gas tank, and angular fenders.

On the other hand, the 1932 Ford boasted gentler, more rounded curves, especially at the fenders and grille shell. Many automotive historians suggest that the Deuce's modern (by 1932 standards) styling was patterned after FoMoCo's Lincoln, the company's luxury line leader. The 1932 Ford, experts point out, was a scaled-down version of the Lincoln, a body design that Edsel Ford also supervised.

Regardless of what experts say about the 1932 Ford and its impact on automotive history, the Deuce has become a legend among hot rodders the world over. No other car embodies the spirit of hot rodding the way the Deuce can and does. Its finely sculpted lines, its smooth, aerodynamic grille shell, and the gracefully curved frame have made the 1932 Ford a stand-out car for hot rodding. It's been that way ever since the days when the Ford flathead V-8 ruled the roost, and it will probably remain so for years to come. Life treats you that way when you reside at the top of the food chain.

River City Reliability Run

Racing wasn't the only activity that pioneer hot rodders enjoyed with their cars. They also participated in reliability runs, which were events run on public roads and highways. The purpose of a reliability run was to challenge the hot rodders' driving and navigating skills. It also gave them a chance to see just how reliable their hot rods were under daily driving conditions.

Reliability runs were especially popular immediately after World War II. In order to conserve fuel and materials during the war, the U.S. government had suspended all forms of racing. When peace was declared in 1945, many of the race associations remained in a state of limbo until former club members could reorganize to get their activity agendas back up to speed, in a manner of speaking.

Compared to staging a race, however, organizing a reliability run was rather easy. To promote a reliability run, all a hot rod club had to do was map out a route for participants to follow

Just like the old days, the hot rodders gather at the start for the River City Reliability Run. And, just like the old days, the cars are based on traditional-styled hot rods.

An open-top, highboy Model T, fat whitewall tires, and the wind in your face. Pete and Carol Chapouris experience what some people can only dream about.

over public roads and highways, issue a set of instructions for drivers and their navigators to follow, then tabulate the scores at the conclusion of the event. Scoring was based on how close the finishers' times were in relation to an average speed that the organizers had previously established. Bonus points were given if your hot rod finished in a "reliable" manner.

One of the more popular runs was sanctioned by the Pasadena Roadster Club (PRC). First held in 1947, the PRC run originated at the famous Rose Bowl football stadium. From there, it traversed the nearby San Gabriel Mountains, meandered through the Mojave Desert on the northeast side of the mountain range before terminating at a location about 130 miles from the start. Because the PRC was a chapter of the Southern California Timing Association, initial runs were restricted to roadster hot rods only. Other clubs promoted reliability runs for closed-top cars, and for the next several years this was a popular form of competition among nonracing hot rodders.

The reliability runs eventually faded from the hot rod scene, but the term "run" remained a part of the hot rodders' vocabulary for the subsequent decades. Eventually, however, the runs turned into social affairs rather than driving exercises, because hot rodders acquired the habit of parking their cars at a run site so peo-

ple could check out their hot rods. Once the hot rods were parked, the run turned more into a social event or bench-racing session.

One southern California hot rodder decided it was time for sedentary hot rodders — who had resigned themselves to parking their lawn chairs — to get back in the driver's seat, so they could enjoy their hot rods for what they were built for — driving. So Mark Morton organized the River City Reliability Run to be run in the spirit of the old Pasadena Run. The first River City Run was held December 1995 in Riverside, California.

The inaugural River City Reliability Run was by invitation only, and open only to hot rods that were based on traditional styling trends. The emphasis was on two things: driving and hot rod nostalgia. As Morton's flyer stated for his first event: "Yeah, just like the Pasadena Roadster deal in the late '40s & '50s. Traditional hot rods only! No billet! No high-tech, etc. Real rods with steelies and all that."

More than 50 entries showed up for the first River City Run. And each hot rod was, as Morton prescribed, based on the traditional styles that were so prevalent when the Pasadena Roadster Club promoted its first event nearly a half century before.

The legend of Stroker McGurk lives on in Dave Lukkari's Ardun-powered modified-T roadster.

CHAPTER 4

The Wonder Years: 1933-1940

HOT RODDING GROWS AND MATURES

F rom an economic standpoint, what occurred in the auto industry during the height of the Great Depression doesn't make sense. On the national level car sales were down, unemployment was up, yet throughout the 1930s some auto makers in America continually expanded their range of new models.

New-car sales in America for model-year 1929— the months immediately preceding the collapse of the stock market—topped 5,294,000. By 1933—four years after the world fell into economic darkness— that figure diminished to only 1,848,000. The auto industry was not without its victims. One-third of the auto makers went bankrupt during that brief period. They were joined by

Doug Kenny rescued this Model 40 coupe in the seventies. "But," said Kenny about the 1934, "it had been around for quite a while before I bought it." The five-window sports some old-fashioned, rod-building tricks, too, including independent front suspension from a 1954 Chevrolet and an Oldsmobile rear end. The body boasts some vintage styling treatments, too, right down to the 2 1/2-inch chopped top and the front and rear tubular steel nerf bars.

Not all hot rods are coupes and roadsters. Warren Hokinson spent more than three decades collecting parts for his 1935 pickup, which he built in 1990. The clean-looking pickup has a 300-cubic-inch flathead V-8 for power. The remainder of the drivetrain is based around a 1946 Lincoln transmission mated to a Columbia overdrive rear end. "Hoke" bought the truck in 1949. He paid $115.

an equally long list of insolvent suppliers and wholesalers. Practically overnight one of the largest industries in the country was on its knees and showing signs of further collapse.

Despite the worldwide economic turmoil and the hard times the population was enduring, the auto makers focused on expanding new model availability. The 1932 Ford product line featured no less than 14 different models, ranging from the least-expensive roadster to the high-end Deluxe Ford convertible sedan. Within the next nine years Ford expanded its product line to include three distinct trim levels: Standard, Deluxe, and Super Deluxe. By 1941 a customer — providing he or she

had the money — could walk into a Ford dealership and order a convertible coupe (the more rudimentary roadster was dropped after the 1937 model), sedan, or convertible sedan in at least one of these three variations.

For the most part, auto stylists were issued orders to change body features on an annual basis. The 1932 Ford — the Deuce — was a one-year style, followed by an all-new design that lasted only two years: the 1933 and 1934 twins. Despite more than 100 model changes for 1934, the 1933 and 1934 models are mainly distinguished from each other by the 1933's more shovel-shaped grille. Finally, for 1935, Ford once and for all entered the yearly styling cycle with completely revamped body lines, even though the chassis and running gear remained basically unchanged from 1934.

The 1936 Ford had even more definitive lines. Because it successfully created a new and interesting style, the 1936 has remained a favorite among hot rodders. The 1935 and 1936 Fords shared pretty much the same chassis, however, and their body structures were similar enough that hot rodders could mount a 1936 grille and hood onto a 1935 and have what was deemed a cool-looking car.

For 1937 Ford stylists showed what they had learned about streamlining, placing the headlights in the front fenders rather than on top of them. Despite the 1937 Ford's more fanciful styling, for many years hot rodders considered it and the slightly fatter 1938 the ugly ducklings of the Ford family. It was not until the late 1980s that the 1937 became an accepted body style for hot rodding. Contrarily, the 1939 and 1940 — both years shared the same basic Deluxe styling treatment, although their stainless steel trim differs — have always been well received, by regular Ford customers and hot rodders alike. When discussing the merits of collecting various Fords, one enthusiast magazine described the ever-popular 1940 this way: "Good looks make the '40 a sales leader, and the '40's fantastic survival rate is probably for the same reason."

Some people pay hundreds of thousands of dollars for a hot rod. Martin Williams was willing to spend "between $5,000 and $6,000" to build this 1936 pickup. He helped keep costs down using a stock bore-and-stroke 1947 flattie. The 239 motor has a Thickston dual-carb manifold, Howard M14-grind cam, and Edelbrock heads. The remainder of the drivetrain is old-timey, too: a 1939 trans with 1947 gears, 1940 Ford rear end, and 15-inch Ford wheels mounted with wide-whites. Check out the white tonneau cover and light-blue pinstripes.

With availability of such a diverse group of new Ford models, hot rodding and custom car building in the 1940s and early 1950s experienced marked changes from previous years. As it happened, this was the era in which hot rodders began to accept coupes and sedans as worthy candidates for hot rodding. When the SCTA (Southern California Timing Association) was formed November 29, 1937, one of its bylaws excluded closed-top cars from competing at dry lakes meets. The belief among early-day rodders was that the racing should be open only to hot rods. Because most hot rods during that era were roadsters, chances were favorable that any closed-top car (coupe or sedan) showing up on race day was probably a "stocker." Rather than waste time determining whether or not a car was truly modified for competition, the SCTA members simply limited the racing to open-top cars.

That dictum changed shortly after racing resumed during the postwar years, and eventually hot rodders began showing greater interest in coupes and sedans. One racer who helped open the door to integration among the two factions was Don Brown of the Russetta Timing Association (RSA). The RSA allowed coupes and sedans to race at their meets, and when Don Brown steered his 1936 Ford five-window coupe through the lights at 120-plus miles per hour, the guys from the SCTA raised their eyebrows, doubting the RSA's accuracy in timing. The only solution was to invite Brown to El Mirage so he could race his 1936 coupe through the SCTA timing lights. Brown showed up for the August 28–29, 1948, meet, where he ran 121.68 miles per hour. The myth was broken—hard-top cars could be hot rods too.

Stepping into this truck's interior is like stepping back in time. Owner Martin Williams maintained the Spartan flavor of a pickup, using a set of Stewart Warner gauges, gennie floor shift, 1936 Ford banjo steering wheel and rolled and pleated Naugahyde upholstery. The pinstriping on the glovebox is a nice touch.

The thing that caught Hal Peterson's attention about this 1938 convertible was its Carson top. "It's a real Carson top," he pointed out, "chopped, formed and padded the way they used to make them in the early days of customizing." Peterson isn't certain about the car's lineage, but there's no denying that this blue cruiser depicts the early days. Check it out: full fender skirts, flipper wheel covers, frenched license plate holder, original Appleton spotlights, and lacquer paint.

Another catalyst that helped change the myth was the maturity level of the hot rodders. By 1948, many of the experienced rodders were older (and wiser), and more willing to trade a little comfort for the accepted "look" of a roadster (keep in mind a roadster lacked creature comforts such as roll-up side windows and a heater—amenities that could be found in most coupes and sedans). And so cars of all styles began showing up at the southern California dry lakes shortly after the war, and at the Salt Flats in 1949 for the inaugural Bonneville Nationals.

The coupes and sedans also found favor among the street crowd; the modifications usually were for cosmetic purposes rather than to the engine. An example of a typical hot rod during that era was a particular 1936 Ford three-window coupe owned by Bob Poe. His custom treatment back in 1938 included fender skirts, flipper wheel covers, an inverted-V center section on the rear bumper (the tail-mounted spare tire was removed), and filled-in hood skirts. Recalls Poe today, "That's how we made them back in those days."

Poe's car wasn't all show and no go. He proved it at Muroc Dry Lake before the war when he made a top-speed run of 90-plus miles per hour. At that time you were among the elite when you made the 90 Mile An Hour Club. Poe still owns the bumper plaque that was presented to him by the timing association. He was member number 10.

Despite the growing popularity of the hard-head hot rods, the street crowd didn't abandon their beloved roadsters, as evidenced by a letter-to-the-editor that appeared in the first issue of *Rods & Customs* magazine, published in the spring of 1953 (as of the second issue the magazine's name was changed to its current title: *Rod & Custom*). The letter, penned by

Hal Peterson bought this 1938 convertible from Vern Williams in 1983. A short time later he re-upholstered the interior himself, using tan Naugahyde. The '40 Ford column and shifter were chromed, as was the entire dashboard and window garnish mouldings.

Most die-hard hot rodders will agree: 1940 Fords were meant for flames. Tom Clark didn't let those die-hards down. As a sign painter and pinstriper, Tom is used to working with graphics, so his 1940 Tudor boasts the full ensemble—flames and stripes, all the work of Tom's own brush. Adding to the cool look is a low stance and classic Ford wheels dressed with 1946 Ford caps and rings.

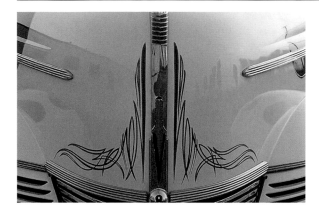

The 1940 Ford Deluxe Tudor's stainless steel trim looks perfect when it's surrounding sheetmetal is smothered in flames and stripes.

R&C reader Ron Weiskind, described a typical, daily-driver hot rod of the period:

"My home is in Seattle where I am a member of the Seattle Kustom Club. Please find enclosed a few pictures of my car, a 1935 Ford roadster. The fenders, hood, and grill [sic] are from a '36 Ford, the dash is from a '40 Ford, and the bumpers were taken from a '49 Plymouth.

"The engine is a '46 Merc and it is ported and relieved. The bore is 1/4 inch over stock and the stroke has been increased by 5/16 inch. It used big valves, a Winfield 3/4 cam, a Spaulding [sic] dual ignition and a chopped flywheel. The zephyr [sic] gears are actuated by a column shift and I have recently installed hydraulic brakes."

Indeed, the cars that Ford built from 1933 through 1940 helped usher in new and innovative ideas to hot rodding. During the immediate prewar years, Ford introduced several landmark changes to the flathead V-8 that hot rodders would embrace. Foremost were horsepower gains, starting with the jump to 75 horsepower for 1933. Subsequent increases included 85 horsepower in 1934 and the 95-horsepower flathead intended for FoMoCo's new Mercury line of cars in 1939. The Mercury flathead interchanged with the Ford cars in every way. Hot rodders also discovered the close-ratio gear cluster from a Lincoln Zephyr readily bolted into the 1939 Ford top-loader transmission, offering transmission gear ratios better-suited for their performance needs.

Other flathead changes having demonstrative impacts on hot rodding were improved cooling for 1938 and introduction of the more rugged 24-stud head the following year. Perhaps the biggest improvement that Ford made to its cars was the use of hydraulic brake systems starting with the 1939 model. These juice brakes readily interchanged with earlier Ford wheel spindles and axles, so hot rodders could build their cars to stop as efficiently as they accelerated. It was not uncommon then—and now—to see a 1932 highboy roadster equipped with a set of juice brakes from a 1940 Ford.

These and other less celebrated advancements in the Ford product line helped change the face of hot rodding during the immediate postwar years. It is popularly noted that "change is good." And in the case of hot rodding during the late forties and early fifties, changes that emanated from Dearborn a decade earlier during the Great Depression were, to be sure, very good. Never before did so many changes (actually improvements) have such a profound effect on hot rodding as those resulting from the wonder years of 1933–1940.

Years ago blue-dot taillights were a no-no in most states. Today many state legislatures have given them the green light. Say today's law makers, "Nostalgia is cool."

L.A. Roadsters Show

A s the name suggests, the L.A. Roadsters Club is an organization that, for more than 40 years, has devoted itself expressly to hot rod roadsters. And every Father's Day weekend the L.A. Roadsters promote the L.A. Roadsters Exhibition, Trade Show and Swap Meet at the Pomona Fairplex in southern California. Many nationally sanctioned rod runs easily surpass the L.A. Roadsters Show for sheer volume of entries, but there's no disputing that the annual Father's Day gathering of top-down hot rods ranks as one of rodding's finest hours.

First held in 1960 at the Hollywood Bowl, this event has become the crown jewel for hot rod enthusiasts who feel that there is really only one kind of hot rod—roadsters. And for two days every year the Pomona Fairplex is overrun with hot rod roadsters, convertibles, and cabriolets. The number of entries grows annually, and today it's not uncommon for more than 500 of the finest open-top hot rods to show up and show off.

The show itself has a colorful history, too. The initial roadster round-ups were held at the Hollywood Bowl parking lot, and by the early 1970s the event shifted to the Great Western Exhibition Center in Los Angeles. The L.A. Roadsters relocated a third and final time in 1980 to the Pomona Fairplex.

Throughout the years, though, one thing remains constant: The show continues to spotlight roadsters, where you'll find only open-top cars in the main arena. Coupes, sedans, and trucks are relegated to a separate parking lot that, by comparison, can be considered a sideshow when compared to the main attraction. There's also a manufacturer's midway where vendors hawk their new rodware. A special section remains devoted for swap meet sellers and buyers who maintain the time-honored hot rod practice of recycling old car parts.

But most of all, the L.A. Roadsters Show is a favorite and a must-go because it brims with enthusiasm—by the club members who put on the show, the guest car owners who display their hot rods, and the spectators who revel in the beauty the topless cars have to offer.

And it's this enthusiasm that has carried the L.A. Roadsters Show through the years, building it into what it is today — one of the premier events on the hot rod calendar. No doubt there will be plenty more L.A. Roadsters Shows to follow. But you won't find any of them playing at your neighborhood theater, unless, of course, you happen to live in Southern California, where this show opened back in 1960.

Held annually on Father's Day weekend, the L.A. Roadsters Show is about hot rod roadsters, and about fathers and sons enjoying those hot rod roadsters.

Ford Hot Rods are Forever

A UNIVERSE OF RODDING OPTIONS

T radition, according to one dictionary, is defined as "...customs and usages viewed as a coherent body of precedents influencing the present." As such, traditional-style Ford hot rods built today should—and do—resemble those that emerged from pioneer hot rodders' garages 50, even 60, years ago. Yet, while there can be marked resemblances between today's traditional hot rods and the "originals" that were built decades ago, the growth cycle has spawned innovations and developments that, through the years, actually improved this particular form of hot rod.

Generally speaking—from a technical and engineering standpoint—today's traditional-style hot rods have improved, but cosmetically there is little

Mark Morton's low-slung 1929 highboy has the look of a traditional hot rod. You'd know that there's a classic Chevy 327 V-8 sitting under the hand-formed hood. The roadster boasts a wealth of styling tricks such as 1933 Ford hood-skirt louvers to accent the Model A's classy cowl curve, reshaped upper cowl section to conform to the DuVall-style windshield, a Carson-style top, and a chopped '32 Ford grille.

The tri-power carburetion—a trio of Rochester two-barrels—looks elegant when contrasted to the 1933 Ford curved hood-side louvers.

differentiation between old and new examples. Consequently, treatment to the body, interior, and wheels and tires remains much the same today as in the early years.

Many of the building techniques for a truly authentic traditional-style hot rod remain the same, too. For example, when fitting a Model A hot rod with a Ford flathead V-8 (this hybrid is known as an A-V8), purists still modify a 1932 K-member to fit the Model A frame. And a quick method to lower a Deuce hot rod is to use a Model A front cross-member, while Model A rear cross-members are typically used when fitting Halibrand V-8 quick-change rear ends to '32 Fords. Juice brakes from 1940–1948 Fords are still common transplants to

older mechanical-brake Fords. And most flathead V-8 rebuilds today still rely on a wealth of early-day speedware. It's not uncommon, however, to see a 12-volt generator spliced into the electrical charging system for improved starting and sparking.

Despite the popularity that early-Ford running gear still enjoys among traditionalists, late-model, overhead-valve engines, and modern transmissions and rear-axle members also are acceptable equipment on many of today's nostalgia-styled hot rods. Perhaps the most popular update is the use of a Chevrolet small-block V-8 for power. Ironically, shortly after Chevrolet introduced this overhead valve V-8 in 1955, it became the engine of choice among many hot rodders seeking more horsepower for their cars. Simply, the Chevrolet engine's modern design offered more performance potential than was available from the outdated flathead V-8, or even Ford's new Y-block overhead-valve motor introduced in 1954. When two of General Motors' divisions—Cadillac and Oldsmobile—offered their cutting-edge overhead-valve V-8s in 1949, the flathead V-8—a dinosaur by comparison—already was heading down that lonesome trail to extinction. Two years later Chrysler came out with its hemi-spherical-head V-8, and within a few years Buick and Pontiac joined the V-8 club, too. These and other engines led to the flathead abdicating as hot rodding's power king. A wide assortment of speed equipment for the Chevy small-block further led to the dethronement of the aging Ford motor.

The flathead V-8 wasn't the only portion of the drivetrain destined to be replaced by new, more modern ware. By the 1960s, old Ford three-speed "top-loader" transmissions were routinely finding

This Model A roadster, owned by Joe Scanlin, was the third of three similar roadsters built by the late Dick Courtney. The styling is straightforward, even simple in execution, yet very seductive thanks to its classic composition of a 1929 body on Deuce rails. The powertrain is all late-model stuff, based on a Chevy 350 small-block, Muncie four-speed transmission, and Currie-built Ford 9-inch rear end. The windshield isn't a DuVall screen, either; this particular bug catcher was designed by early-day hot rod legend Duke Hallock.

their way onto garage floors, replaced by more sophisticated four-speed trannies from companies like Muncie and Borg-Warner. Early-Ford rear axles, too, were shelved in place of a newer, stronger third-member from Ford—the 9-inch rear end, first used in 1957. Drag racers were the first to recognize the potential of this near-bullet-proof third member. Later, hot rodders adopted it as the ultimate rear end for street use, mainly because Ford supplied the 9-inch with a wide assortment of gears that allow car builders to tailor-fit tire and transmission combinations with suitable final-drive ratios.

Eventually hot rodders began improving their cars' chassis, incorporating independent front and rear suspensions for improved ride and more precise handling. Corvette and Jaguar independent rear suspension systems were especially popular during the seventies, while the late-fifties hot rods sprouted

Bill Nielsen's modified-T roadster has a refined Model A four-cylinder for power. The four-banger has a Winfield cam and Mallory dual-point system. The Winfield "crow's foot" cylinder head is a reproduction offered by Antique Auto, and the two Winfield BU carbs were converted to be sidedrafts. The old-time headers were modified to conform to the frame, which happens to be made of 2-inch-by-3-inch steel tubing.

A side view of Mike Armstrong's Model A shows classic lines, even though the engine and body are new reproductions.

independent front suspension packages that were grafted from various postwar-era cars. A popular independent front suspension adaptation among hot rodders at that time was to mount the front suspenders from a 1953–54 Chevrolet onto 1933-and-later Fords. By the seventies entire bolt-on kits became available, using spindles, A-arms, even rack-and-pinion steering systems from Mustang IIs and Pintos. These conversions also conveniently incorporated disc brakes for the hot rods that used them.

Still, there were die-hard hot rodders who opted to retain solid-axles on their cars. They, too, could upgrade their otherwise obsolete suspension systems with four-bar locators. As the name suggests, the four bar system uses four bars—two on each side of the axle—that are adjustable to align the axle and hold it in place. This design originally was perfected on race cars, and to this day remains popular among many street-bound hot rods. Traditionalists, however, still opt for either the split wishbones or hairpin radius rods that were popular in the early days of hot rodding.

Regardless of the innovations, most traditionalist hot rod fans today are more interested in maintaining the early-style look, as opposed to mechanical-correctness, for their hot rods. Even if a new Chevrolet 350 small-block or an older GM overhead-valve V-8 is plopped in front of the fire-

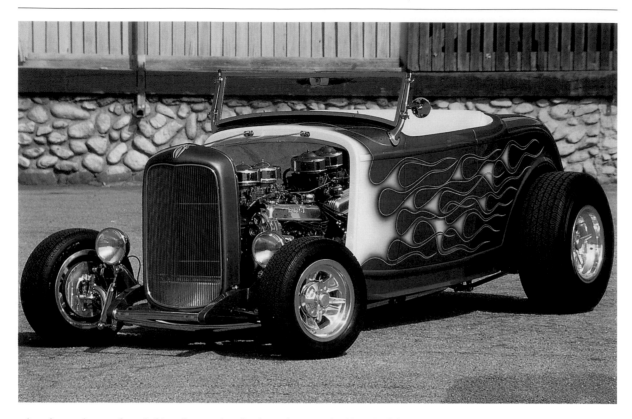

The aftermarket is rife with fiberglass replica bodies. This 1932 highboy built by Gary Moline has a Gibbon body on a TCI chassis. Gary wanted the powerplant to stand out, so he elected to use a 401 "nailhead" Buick V-8. Add flames, and you have one cool ride.

wall, or a four-speed overdrive automatic transmission and rebuilt 9-inch rear end completes the drivetrain, the hot rod's overall physical appearance can—and usually does—mirror that of hot rodding's glory days when men wore button-top caps and hot rods wore white wall tires.

This popularity has led to a burgeoning aftermarket industry that specializes in early-Ford reproduction parts. Demand is booming, and the aftermarket is saturated with enough "re-pop" parts that an enthusiast today can build a traditional-style hot rod using all-new parts. That includes bodies and chassis, complete drivetrains, even bolt-on goodies such as wheels and tires, headlights and taillights, and chopped windshield posts.

Based on the variety of reproduction parts, and the acceptance of non-Ford powerplants, today it's possible to build an entire traditional hot rod simply by shopping from a catalog. True, the end product is not an authentic nostalgia-rod, but it does, nonetheless, reflect an era of hot rodding that was challenging and exciting to all who experienced it.

We mustn't kid ourselves, the early days of hot rodding can never be relived. But, thanks in large part to the hard work and enthusiasm of dedicated hobbyists across the country, hot rodding's early era can certainly be remembered for what it was—a time of tinkering, exploring and learning. These Ford hot rods represent a tradition that enthusiasts hope will last forever.

The "nailhead" Buick engine in Gary Moline's 1932 highboy reflects a time when hot rodders relied on ingenuity and the parts at hand to build their cars.

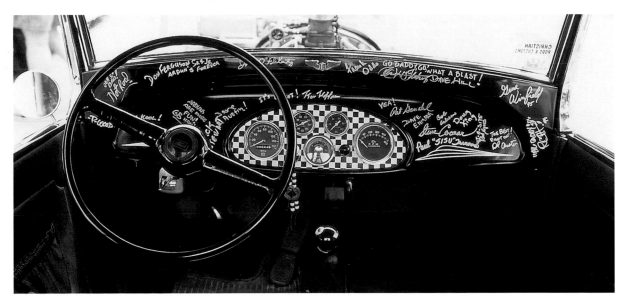

The dashboard on Dave Lukkari's funky 1928 modified Model T is dressed with signatures from many of today's hot rod legends. Their presence and conviction to hot rodding reaffirm our belief, and that is—hot rod Fords are forever!

NHRA California Hot Rod Reunion

Promote it and they will come. "They" are nostalgia drag racers and hot rodders, and every November nostalgia returns for a pass down drag racing's memory lane when the National Hot Rod Association (NHRA) holds its annual California Hot Rod Reunion at one of the oldest tracks in America, Famoso Raceway near Bakersfield, California. Famoso—better known to old-timers as Bakersfield Raceway, home of the Smoker's Car Club—hosts the Reunion so that drag racers and hot rodders from all eras gather to talk and reminisce about yesteryear. Not to be left out, there's also a full card of racing that includes nostalgia classes for front-engine top fuel dragsters, junior fuelers, altereds, and selected support classes.

But the main thrust behind the Hot Rod Reunion takes place behind the bleachers where hot rod buffs young and old can

Bakersfield Raceway used to be home of the Smoker's March Meet, where the Top Fuelers squared off every year to see who was king of the smoke. Today nostalgia fills the air at Bakersfield when the NHRA promotes its annual Hot Rod Reunion.

It's not Ford powered, but who really cares? The Glass Slipper is such a beautiful fifties-dragster that it's worth a stare.

mingle, and appreciate the sport's past rather than its future. For that reason, hundreds of old hot rods and dragsters are trailered to Bakersfield where, for two days, everyone in the pits gets an eye-full, an ear-full, even a nose-full of prime-time hot rodding. Because once you pass through the gates to the Reunion, the nostalgia intoxicates your senses, making you feel as though you just took a giant whiff of a smoking M&H Racemaster slick during a sizzling burn-out.

The nostalgia high that you'll enjoy is nothing short of sensational. On the drag strip the top fuelers are nipping at 5-second passes, with top speeds in the 220-mile-per-hour range. There are several exhibition runs down the quarter-mile steel gauntlet too. Cars like the late "Wild" Willie Borsch's Winged Express AA/Fuel Altered fries its huge slicks as it launches viciously off the starting line, or wheel-stand passes by such legends as the Hurst Hemi Under Glass or the Red Fire Engine.

Back in the pits, there's always something interesting to see because that's where the celebrity cars are parked along Nostalgia Row behind the bleachers. There you'll see all sorts of famous hot rod race cars; any one of Mickey Thompson's Challengers could show up, not to forget Tony Nancy's infamously clean orange roadsters, or Art Chrisman's famed Hustler I. The smooth

and svelte Glass Slipper, a fifties-era slingshot dragster, is a regular attraction, too. Nearby there's a vendor's row where you can buy nostalgic hot rod products and souvenirs, plus a swap meet that caters to buyers shopping for old hot rod parts and accessories. At the other end of the parking lot, the promoters cordon a special area open only to hot rods and customs belonging to enthusiast spectators attending the meet.

The Reunion also abounds with hot rod celebrities from the past. And if you don't really know who to look for, then be near the start line on Saturday when the NHRA inducts several honorees into the Hot Rod Reunion Hall of Fame. Some of the past inductees include drag racing's First Lady, Linda Vaughn; former Top Fuel and Funnycar driver, Don Prudhomme; "TV" Tommy Ivo; and one of the original Bean Bandits, Joaquin Arnett.

The California Hot Rod Reunion has been described by one NHRA official as "a romantic thing." Perhaps NHRA founder Wally Parks summed it up best when he once said about the Reunion: "That's what real reunions are all about—people remembering and appreciating good times. And that is why we're back again this year, at the Bakersfield Smoker's legendary old stomping ground where, like hundreds of other locations across the country, a lot of hot rodding history has its roots."

INDEX